The Richard Poems

Elizabeth Clayton

Order this book online at www.trafford.com
or email orders@trafford.com

Most Trafford titles are also available at major online book retailers.

Printed in the United States of America.

ISBN: 978-1-4269-6992-8 (sc)
ISBN: 978-1-4269-6993-5 (e)

Trafford rev. 06/27/2011

 www.trafford.com

North America & International
toll-free: 1 888 232 4444 (USA & Canada)
phone: 250 383 6864 ♦ fax: 812 355 4082

Foreword

I am flattered that Betty has asked me to write the foreword to her book of poetry dedicated to her late husband. However, I'm sure her poetry will mean different things to different people. I enjoy it but can only look at it through the prism of my knowledge of my friends, Betty and her husband Richard, viewed from the vantage point of nearly 50 years.

I want to share the background of my relationship with these two friends because I feel it may provide some insight into Betty's poetry.

Betty's husband, Richard, and I became friends in college and I became close to Betty when they began dating. They were very open about problems with Richard's physical health and Betty's mental health. Being able to share these concerns contributed to a closer relationship between us. At the time I was a very successful young executive with a large advertising agency in Jackson. I invited them to enjoy the good life with me and we did, on many occasions. Then, my position abruptly changed.

I was out of work, humiliated and despondent. Richard and Betty were my most supportive friends during that bleak period.

I mention this because I felt that having gone through so much together, I knew pretty much all that close friends would know about each other. The fact that we knew each other so well made any kind of pretensions laughable.

Yet, as I was to learn from Betty's poetry, there existed a very private and intimate, parallel side of their relationship I could have no way of knowing. Looking back, there were a few clues but never enough to come to any conclusion.

One such missed opportunity occurred early along in their marriage. Two close friends from our college days, Luke and Marlene Dove, were as aware as I that we were losing touch with Richard and Betty. Very concerned, they proposed that we take them out to dinner. All agreed that it was an excellent idea and arrangements were made at one of our favorite restaurants.

Luke, Marlene and I arrived and waited on our dinner guests. The better part of an hour passed before Richard and Betty breezed in, rosy cheeked, laughing and clearly inebriated, as though they had just come from a festive party. They made only the most casual reference about being late and totally immersed in their own personal conversation, completely unaware of our attempts to engage them.

They remained in their own impenetrable world, fascinated with each other and eager to excuse themselves into the evening as soon as they could do without leaving unfinished food behind.

My friends and I were stunned. Richard and Betty had always conducted themselves in the most gracious and entertaining manner. This aberration was completely inexplicable to us. We attributed it to their drinking, although that was not uncommon at the time and had never affected in that way before.

It was only through reading Betty's poetry, over a quarter century later, that I realized we had met their alter selves, Sir Harold and Lady Agatha. This role playing permitted them to assume different personas and step outside the stresses of marriage and illness they faced.

I have been the fortunate recipient of Betty's poetry for many years. There is almost always an envelope, sheaf or book of it nearby anywhere in my home.

For me, Betty's poetry has always evoked the sensation of a flower garden, filled with the images she loves to write and paint. Ever-present are her blossoming gardenias, carnations and roses. Words describe honeysuckle and jasmine as well giving them sweet aroma and covering them with dew. Eucalyptus, ivy and all sorts of foliage provide a rich texture for changes from night to day, season to season and connect with the range of human emotion.

However, at least in my mind, the garden analogy becomes far more complex as she examines her evolving relationship with her husband, Richard, both during his life and following his death. We realize that a garden also contains weeds, briers and thorns that can thrive if the garden is not properly tended.

My analogy operates at several levels, including The Garden from the book of Genesis.

Also, there is Betty's own very real garden which she tends compulsively, often at 3:00 in the morning to avoid the heat of the day. She fully understands what it takes to cultivate flowers as well and write about them and paint them.

Then there is the level of that euphemism for the graveyard, a Garden of Memories. This one contains lots of bones, and, even the Garden of Good and Evil. She makes no judgments but neither does she avoid any consequences.

Betty takes the reader on a journey that begins with Richard leading her meekly along the garden's path. Her mental illness renders her totally dependent. However, as they work their way through the marital garden, she learns and grows painfully as Richard's disease and demons bring him down. In the end, it is her strength that guides them through the labyrinth they themselves have created.

Richard's death does not end the journey but simply marks the second phase of continuing examination of loss. Betty's poetry faithfully records the way mourning, grief and illusion evolve over the years and the different ways she comes to terms with it at each stage.

That is my vantage point. I found far more in Betty's book of poetry that I ever expected. No doubt you will read and hear something very different than I. But, wherever your perspective takes you, I have no doubt that you will find a very special read.

I just hope you can experience some of the surprise and pleasure that I enjoyed.

Marketin Miller
June 2011

TABLE OF CONTENTS

To all who have at some time truly loved,

whatever its fashioning, and keep a residual sweetness,

whatever its portion, be it flavored of julep or

lightly of absinthe –

Elizabeth
May 5, 2011
Near Midnight

Acknowledgements

When preparing acknowledgement remarks for a completed work, the author usually expresses gratitude for interest, encouragement, and often substantial effort. In the matter of this piece, a written work, it was I, alone, who "beat my music out," speaking of and to my late husband, of my many and varied feelings which were, at least, half its fire that consumed our love. No one knew the fifteen years of writing, heard or read their sentiments except one of Richard's high school instructors, and dear friend, Jonah Ford, and my devoted nephew, Jason. The first source, however, of most vital support, came from my physician and friend, Dr. John Norton, who continued, always, to encourage me to write and place my husband in the full tapestry that has woven out as my life.

And then, several years ago, I became reacquainted with one of Richard's fraternity brothers, Jim Miller, who has continued to be interested and encouraging concerning my poetry, reading great portions of it, as well as my prose work. He has offered compliments and many helpful, well-thought suggestions, especially about this piece for which he graciously prepared the foreword.

Finally there is my able and constant companion and friend, Ora Steele, who sees that thought is alive on the page, careful in all such matters.

To these four, I offer words of sincere gratitude, my fullest appreciation. We all speak of love, but we five, together, have made it possible to experience, in some manner of worded, thoughtful sentiment, the convoluted bramble of love and relationship, which stands, modestly, as an expression, a worthy manifestation, of a true measure of humanity.

Elizabeth

May 6, 2011

four-ten am

Preface

Preparing preface remarks for a work, no matter its specific qualities, is always a thoughtful venture. Some are more easily composed than others, and there are myriads of variables that enter the circumstance that facilitate or make more difficult the effort necessary to the completed piece.

I have written some few prefaces, to my earlier published works, and I come, now, to the most challenging one, simply because it is explanation to the longest, most intense relationship of my life, other than that of the years with my immediate family. To add to the challenge it brings is, that in a reflective stance (although I was partially aware as I lived through it), I am cognizant, now, fully, that it was an arrangement in which a relationship played out, through, at the first, mutual care and dependencies, to become a pathological script of most complicated proportions.

Care and passion, jaundiced by poor identity and selfhood, inordinate dependence and illness, with anger inside it; clever and exaggerated mechanisms toward adjustment, growing competition as failures to succeed in the wished goal accumulated; the slow dying of genuine affection through repeated, confused negative behaviors; the loss of the ability to listen alongside abject denial, and the eroding forbearance to forgive; the transfer of inadequacies, including infidelities of sorted arrangements, on both our parts – finally to desperate isolation and alienation with the wish to be free, but also with too great fear to take definitive action – and somehow, residual loyalty that followed its thread of faithfulness the full distance back to the first thousand white gardenias in small bedrooms, full with summer heat – this final quality in the relationship compounds and drapes the entire record in verse with a poignancy that touches me yet, even after the diminishing of the using one another's lessening strengths in the face of personal inadequacies and insecurities, together with lost, simple courtesies and former honesty and honor.

All of the verses included in the volume, and they comprise all that are extant, which I penned, other than some several that only reference him(as the 'Hammack' verse), and do not speak of him in the verse's full -- these pieces were written, in greatest part, in the fifteen years after my husband's death in 1992. My mourning was, at times, a mixture of grief expressed of other losses, but most for a dream that could, now, never be recaptured, the illusion that it had been in completeness once – a "Cinderella" symptom which I had difficulty with putting aside. I mourned, also, the years, more than twenty, lost to a cause that could never have been won, an enemy that could not be subdued, demons that could not be exorcised. I also grieved at the metamorphosing of my own person, through the long process – the passing of time, the joy of the day, beauty, productivity, the influence of negative thought and behavior – and there was the matter of my own psychiatric illness: andso there is much loss ledgered – those, the verses of the first years, and more.

We tend to speak of relationships in absolute terms; perhaps the matter would be more easily dealt with in that fashion, but people are not "all good," or "all bad," but a beautiful and heinous mixture of the both. We remember the sweetness of gardenias with drunken nights, gifts of garnet stones with scathing statements such as "I liked you better when you were more ill," "my poor country girl," or "used merchandise," and "asset rather than …." And, I was not without my Scarlet. The verse, then, reflects this characteristic of behavior, of Richard, and me, alongside that of our alter selves, Harold and Agatha, or, as I affectionately refer to us, on occasion, Olive and Rose.

There is the progress of expressing of deepest grief toward a gradual putting in place what really was, the lovely and the unlovely. It came in the years following the realization of many elements in the relationship that I either had not known, or had not faced honestly. But time is a great equalizer, putting experience in proper place, despite my bipolar intensity in the effort to "make everything acceptable, as I wanted it."

The later, or latest, verses are sometimes distant, and sometimes, not so much. I had thought, and so written, that I could not ever feel the hurt I once had, or be touched in such manner again, but I have learned that a beautiful, one moment in reality can be bested by the memory or replaying of it. We love, always, in portions, even if the whole no longer exists.

I learned much from Richard, and lost much to him. For the experiences that were good, these gifts, I am appreciative; for those not, I am grateful to be adept at placing at a distance where they seldom now touch me. But I have been fortunate to have had the capacity to feel, evaluate, and find some content.

I gave much to Richard, as he did to me, out our humble resources, and in doing so, grew to fill again the emptinesses with which the "gifts" left me. Fertile became the darknesses and secrets I kept, the charades I walked through. For that exchange, I, again, am grateful, and, more, now happily productive, if with a bittersweetness.

In the matter of the heart, that which we attribute to romantic dressing, I shall never see gardenias, or now enjoy their fragrance, in warmest June, taste true strawberry wine, select his "Pathtetique" for quiet listening and thought, without a rush of tenderness, for this such was the first I had experienced so. We were young, strong of will. And we had good chemistry between us; libidinal energies were plentiful, if at times poorly executed, influenced by lack of response and lethargy or alternations in mood. We were compatible intellectually, and our conversations came to be some of our closest moments, of oneness – and we had our dreams – the slow, but truly hurried falling away, is the shadow over the entire of the verses, over the heart of any woman in such relationship, the circumstance being early or later experience, if there is shared a common weltanschanng, at any age, being attractive, or no – so that in the last days, I often remembered the former, and in synestheaic ecstasy, could smell his body close to mine. In sum, I came to know the beauty of a man and a woman together, in part, but in that part, in full, in dream or reality, a trueness, in beginning, and in closing, a compassionate responsibility.

The verses are descriptive of our full relationship, the gold side and the underside of the leaf, in reflection, with the inaccuracies such allows, from the first hours together (which were never spent apart), through the three years of courtship, and almost twenty-three of marriage, his illness and death, and the aftermath. I speak of him, to him, offer questions, and recount memories; there are some few that suggest reunion. They are all written in free verse, some narratives, and most, simple and sometimes complex lyrics. There are no illustrations, but rather pictures painted with my selected words. There is no judgment, but only true statement, and, hopefully, a clear picture of how spirits, though of beautiful beginning gestures of close kinship, cannot escape the loss, the futility – the tragedy – of the unhealthy needs of self.

Elizabeth

June 15, 2010

The Game

From the first year of our acquaintance, Richard celebrated my birthday with a fine bottle of wine, one of his choosing, since I, at first, had little knowledge of that portion of his world. He always chose a French red, a Chateau Nerf de Pape, and we would, with great ceremony, drink to my health and happiness. These occasions were arranged so that it would be only he and I together. We had met in April, and my birthday is in September; and on that first celebration, I knew a vague presence about the festivities, even though we drank in quite a controlled manner – still an uncomfortable, undefined presence – in the matter of Richard and alcohol.

Quickly, the details were painted in: dinner left uneaten, later and later hours out, almost every night, and when at home, drinking, in a matter of a few years, to stupor. There were anger, bitterness, regrets, insecurities and accusations, leading to quarrels, weeping, confession, and pardons, and very unhealthy games: alcohol – only the greatest manifestation of many grave problems.

But on occasion, not suggested by any one factor, Richard would try, with great effort, to control his already fixed pattern. The mechanism used was – a game: after he had had several drinks, and the time waited, after dinner (on a night when he was home on schedule), he would turn to me and, with a change in tone, ask politely, graciously, with charm and courtesy, "Agatha would you like a glass of wine." And I came to know to say, "Why, Harold, that would be splendid." There was, then, the ritual of identifying the best wine, selecting glasses, opening the wine, with a flourish, the traditional "tasting," and the lovely gesture of man with woman, he pouring, and the first sip, commenting softly about the wine's outstanding qualities.

We would retire to the small sitting room, and begin a long, very congenial, and most stimulating evening of conversation before sleep. We spoke of many things, often the collegiate "eternal questions," significance, honor, love, fidelity, responsibility – and mutual readings often prompted subjects for thought. To be truthful, few subjects of noble quality escaped our discussions. These conversations brought us together, respectfully equal, with close affection, a gentle passion and admiration for each other. They remain the unique point of oneness that was not ever touched in our years together; Harold and Agatha became our alter selves in numerous conversations and profitable dialogue. It was a beautiful pantomime, one in which all negative aspects of our person and relationship escaped the touch of the paltry mundane.

This part of our experience together is most remembered, as the thousand white gardenias I used to enjoy in summer, walking early in the morning from his rooms to mine, his caring for me in those earliest three years before our marriage, and just after I had left the hospital.

Those conversations continued, intermittently, regardless of whatever other factors were in place, until the year before his death. His body was handsome, his mind beautifully able, and his spirit, when he could closet his demons, as the wealth of the fragrance of summer white, summer soft, summer's better than he could be.

Elizabeth
June 24, 2010

First Voice

Prelude

I awoke today, fully,
after many partial awakenings, with relief
to find that light rather than dark did fill my window.
The quiet hours of the night
were passed with difficulty;
I had traveled a great distance,
catching glimpses of my love
and hearing my verse of him.
I thought, then, of how long
his nights and days had been,
and how he despaired.
He found sometimes a respite in his words and ideas,
his dreams and visions,
perhaps too often in the cup.
His most happy escape
he found in donning gestures
and a special manner to ride, briefly, as Sir Harold.
The pain in it–
unkind suitor to my heart!
What songs we sang, what verse we made;
what dreams and truths we explored and discovered.
The breath of all of our blossoms was sweet.
Even so, he wept in his joy,
knowing it was only for a moment.
In the closing,
he mounted with a finishing movement;
Indeed he mounted and rode quite handsomely,

for I had woven it for the tale thusly;
I have, then, the suggestion for his verse:
It shall be appropriately,
"Harold's Song".

December, 1993
Close to Richard, in memory,
the second Christmas (first year)
following his death.

Chanson de Harold

Ah Harold,
Tonight you came to me when I called your name,
in this season that you left me.
I was deep in reverie, and trumpets
and various other horns with multitudes of strings,
all guided me once more to you,
for a beautiful moment, again, when
we were Harold and Agatha together.
I wonder that I continue to feel
and know that you are with me.
I think perhaps that you shared
such great portions of your soul with me,
and I with you, that we are, still.
When we, at first, found each other,
I was a deep, sad color
with great burdens of stillness and quiet,
and you handled my darkened spirit with care
so that I again felt womanly,
and we began the walk back together.
And in these beautiful and blessed days,
it does not matter that memory reminds me
that I did not know
of all your departures and returns
or understand so many unclear, unsure movings.
I do remember the special, small cigars,
and fine port, brandy and Benedictine
after a wintry, afternoon walk;
there was dry wit, and clever, laughing
at the ironies of our lives;

and then there was
the exciting recounting of our days.
Still, I would not have you back again,
for your beauty would be veiled by darkness;
I prefer the brightness I remember.
The flaw of anger, fear, disgust-
or perhaps boredom and fatigue,
born of a great emptiness,
diminished your brightness even early
and you knew and struggled.
It was never more apparent
that when you would read
Quasimodo's line "Noel, Noel,"
and weep.
Oh my brave knight of light and dark;
Oh Harold, Sir Harold.
I could scarce bare,
and it grieves me still, that you did so weep
when Quasimodo cried "Noel, Noel".
So much you opened to me,
but the matter of Quasimodo you left closed to me.
It may be that I can bare your absence
only by not knowing
all of your covered and hidden places.
Your mysteries, the complete riddle,
give me hope of your salvation.
And so in the graciousness
of the present and of grateful memory,
I am,
you are,
and the others also.

We cannot, this season, exchange glasses,
but I will pen a toast
to us,
to all who love,
and have loved:
may we each know one exchange of soul
that allows the reality of forever.

Postlude

The bleeding of the eucalyptus:
ah, are we as the bleeding eucalyptus,
pulling out all but life,
the color, the substance, to fall,
and be permitted to search out
the paths of that which lies below.
Ivy is handsome,
in its simplicity,
but it does not bleed.
And so, there are those of us,
each fair and comely in our own form,
but some with a separateness,
some, perhaps, within this separateness, a beauty,
more rare to be treasured.
For there are those who bleed,
and there are those who do not bleed,
indeed cannot bleed,
lest they loose their souls
not to find again
and regain once more themselves, not to have married,
moments, soul to another.
And we did, together, bleed,
losing ourselves to each other,
leaving me at these moments, in
each rounding of days, to know
fullest grief with your, only,
holding of my heart, in
eternal distance, eternal silence.

Of Aftertime

Who so?
that life with a moment of awareness is aftertime;
I see it, feel it, smell it,
everywhere--
gardenias in summer
and only a remembrance of faith;
honeysuckle and breakfast sounds,
no more as then,
when I walked early from your apartment;
a brown, straight chair is now merely a suggestion
of one on which you often threw my under silks,
generously touched with body dew,
offering wonderful promises.
When I see large hands, men's hands,
the aftertime is hurt so great
that I am unhappily busy
to quiet the recollection of strong hands
which I, childlike, held to cheerfully,
not understanding
that one of the variations of strength,
which is hardness,
was in the clasp;
nor did I know then that a measure of their beauty
Would show later as wear,
in browntones and fatigue.
And there are other hands,
those that, in past times,
cradled mine, with a great tenderness,
all the more dear now,

being gone away.
With reflection I understand
what great effort gave me that tenderness.
A simple comb tonight is surrounded by afterglow;
you sometimes hid such in a bureau drawer;
it was a feminine comb
and you often had guests to your apartment.
How close remembrance places
all that we have loved.
Home night sounds and wind in trees,
like great fans,
leave me to know that all I am,
feel,
be,
is, what was,
and I stumble alone in the aftertime.

Sodom's Apples

The lord of the court has decreed
that I wear silence;
to his feast,
at his table
my tears and words should be unseen and unheard,
for the clown will take my dark words,
my wistful eyes
and with his balls and sticks,
show them his bright colors,
to laugh into my sorrow.
And so, my pen pours out constructions of
nothing,
my palette's rainbow unnoticed;
the lingering splendor of the afternoon flower
cannot speak to my silent pain,
and my dreams
are but beautiful elegies, without dialogue.
I am a gathering of silence,
and no one will hear my silver ring.
I shall stand wanting of the golden ashes
that lie from Sodom's apples.

The "Jesu" Blossom

When I heard our "Jesu" in the afternoon,
I smiled although inside my heart
was breaking.
Perhaps the pain enabled the smile,
and allowed for its poignant day.

I think of flowers at these times,
their blossoms little universes in themselves,
those we can look into, and
see the whole thereof.

Their bright centers push up, and
warm us with their fragrances,
their souls traveling a great
distance to reach their pleasing
blossoms.

Today, Harold, in hearing the "Jesu,"
I offer my smile, my center,
and my fragrance,
the entrance to my universe whose
daily opening and closing
is fraught with the crimsoned
bearing of my grief.

Elizabeth
1993-1994

Could the organ, with its grande
roundness, catch a soul wandering in the darkness, it
may be
that a spirit, yet an Olive lord, handles the rope
holding his robe,
as winding twine; and he wishes, perhaps, with the
assurance of
morning, that he will find an open door, that he may
move, as the
wind-touched flowers in Persephone's garden, to
reach, with a
full purse of feeling, the quiet pain he has left. For
there is within the
folds of eternity's dress a shadow that leans toward,
and circles
about, mortal love.

Early piece, of Richard (Olive)
Elizabeth (Rose)

Of Thee, Always

Should you wish to know, Harold,
I am aware and feel the April we are in,
the month of your birth
and of our coming together,
joining our laughter and darkness.
Since that time,
it has been,
always.

And should it come to thee,
of the grapevine,
that I see it in tender leaf,
and that it has reached up and caught the oak,
to twine about it,
and down to the azalea to rest on it,
I have looked and seen,
since the planting,
always.

If you feel concern
that the spirit behind my own,
my father's marble blue
yet seeks to know and embrace your own,
your chestnut brown,
within the chambers of my heart
and throughout the majestic halls of the earth,
I search,
without reprieve,
always.

And does the twilight,
softening the now imagined colors,
remind me that you will not arrive after six;
and that with my aloneness
comes a hurting ache of sentiments in my heart,
for yes,
of thee, there is only always.

Aftermath

My voice cannot find its song,
and my dreamer is afraid and quiet;
the winds do not anymore catch my sails,
for my warrior
est mort.
His words will not sound to me again,
and it does not matter that the apple and berry
blossom full into their fruits,
for alone of him, there is not any sweetness.
And without the land,
the emerald no longer sponsors the mighty forest,
nor the sapphire the abundant sky.
How much I wish his crimson
in the grey of the day,
his chestnut in the silence of the light's glow.
Instead there is the heavy dirge
that is the day and the night,
for my warrior
est mort.

An early expression of my feelings of loss,
for my "warrior", a fancy, but true
to Richard's earnest effort to continue
with his true pathos,
full –

At the first, my dependence was required;
in the closing it was my strength that carried us,
and in all the years between
was played out the tragedy in our relationship.
There was not the guillotine in the square,
nor malevolent dregs within our rooms,
but we nonetheless sacrificed one,
the other; executed
between us were two souls
that lost their summer.
When the required oppression,
that to render me dependent
without so that your bag of qualities
could be filled handsomely,
when it fell too heavily,
there came to grow in me
the strength to honor the bag,
and then came to grow in me strength
to stand should I not wish to honor it.
The possessive fingers of control were gentle,
and in rare moments of seeing light,
I wept that I helped to close out touches and smiles,
and you groaned at your growing ineptness,
requiring still a larger bag,
allowing a continuous pantomime
throughout a long day.
Our summer hours were thus filled
with the bag being pregnant
with despair, anger, and pity.
And then, like the close of a summer day
that we had overlooked,

you came to accept,
in your malady and fatigue,
your darkness,
my love, my hands to care,
quite free of the bag.
Why had we filled the gossamer bag;
in this awareness I feel touched
by a sinister laughter
out of the great darkness
of a reluctant summer night.

A Valentine Fancy

We will, someday, find each other again,
perhaps when the mourning dove
has become a quiet, happy arrangement of sunlight,
on the side of the rainbow where the colors
are most true and lasting:
we will recognize and touch
at the graceful, perfect altar
that is found in the rainbow's arc;
I will be raven once more,
and you will smile again in your beautiful strength.
We will not in any fashion move or think
that which does not pleasure and refresh the other.
Our love will,
though found in sorrow,
be a work of beauty and goodness,
for it has stood on both sides of the rainbow.
Eternal friendship!
We have loved passionately,
with passion,
in past days,
more of flame than ivory;
but with the windows of forever opened,

we will love with love,
and I shall not anymore weep after sad love songs.

"Do you think you could love me again;
do you think,
would our broken hearts mend;
if we could find love only half what it's been,
then you could love me again."

-Foster and Allen

In the flowing of waters,
in the passing of white clouds;
in the closing of the day
and in questions that fill the night,
all find their fullness in thoughts of you.
Music brings your eyes and smile,
and tears fill up again your absence.
But you are a coverlet about my shoulders,
for love finds plentiful tokens
that suggest your presence;
and olive, rose bends and shadows them,
in celebration, every one.

Harold,
my dear lost Harold,
I thought of you often today,
as though you shadowed my walk,
and thus were with me;
such was a gentle happiness in this portion of my
springtime.
And then,
I wished to pull you from the distance, the shadow, into
myself,
like a comforting, partially hidden treasure.
In a moment of deep quietness,
when fear and despair sounded,
I could not find the knowing qualities in your face and
body,
the features, the eyes and smile, the commanding
grace.
It was as with the swallow:
I wish it to fly, allowing the sweetness of its grace,
if there be a swallow, or the silkworm,
to see it spin its gold,
if there be a silkworm.
I would see Thee, Harold, if thou be.
Perhaps we may offer our petitions and be
acknowledged,
outdistancing a quest of soul within reason, in truth
the musing of the wishful.
For with the hallowed touch of time,
there has come a lessening of pain, but also, a
negligence,

a lack of attention in the care of details that cannot be of consequence.
And so,
as the reality of an unhappy, grey wind, my grief is rekindled,
that I loose what was given to me to soften the first grief.
Ah Harold, beloved Harold
if there is, indeed, a second leave taking, there will be so left so little,
of our conversations and the truths and insight that rose from their fire,
so little left of the strength I felt on your arm.
And if there be so left little,
wilt thou be little left too?
If it must be so,
pull down all the covering of the heavens, to leave an infinite darkness;
let the brightest eye of the blue sky be driven away,
so as to never again allow the day;
And let the winds and seas be reduced to a tired whisper,
should there be a second leave taking.
Then if it be,
I will weep away, on my arm, my love,
so that you will know that the fidelity that grew out of our troth, is still,
until the dying of this moment.
Can being secumb to nothing;
you will walk through light and worlds, and hasten sound;

with honor and a nobility you will converse with
companion souls;
you will smile on true equality and be content in the
truths you find.
Being will not be given over to nothing.
Where in death are you:
in the round and distant organ pieces I hear;
in the touch of autumn's first cool and grey,
leaving early,
fallen leaves to complete their journey;
or perhaps in the shadow finding my cheek
when I stand to observe the redbird
which frequents your grapevine;
surely you are in my tears that accompany the "Jesu",
but nearer to me in these moments are your lips,
full rounded, fresh blush now pale and still.
And so in death there are not smiles,
only remembrance and collections
that offer persuasions of my attention to them
and their representations of my grief.
I have spoken of the glory in the sun,
and of the elegant moon;
of wind touching rows of satin
tied in flowered knots,
and I would wish you in them,
that all might be part of a beautiful adventure.
The better truth
is that silent, slowly promenading daydreams,
uniquiet conversations,
touching old roses
that suggest our first recognition-

within these lie my treasures,
whatever memory will add unto me.
And, more, with memory
there is a fluid darkness,
that slips away as it is recognized.
It may be that you do not, cannot, wish,
but take your place among all souls who watch
but cannot feel their understanding.

Darkened Laughter

I am dark,
and my songs are woven of words
and sentiments that are dark.
There are times when light finds a receptive lodging,
and then my truths are seen more clearly,
but still attended by shadows.
My tears, whether of the eye or the pen,
wrench pieces of hurt out of me.
Unhappily, I am almost lonely
without the darkness that has parted.
And so, I am dark,
without the pain which has flown,
and with that which cannot leave my heart.
An accumulation of grief,
from either wounds visited on me,
or those I have searched out and found,
has marked my soul
so that the only happiness I know
is imaged as a darkened laughter.

A very early piece

Thee and Me

Today, while driving back from Wesson, I saw two
small, yellow butterflies, moving gracefully among the
bright September sunflowers and green background
of the roadside. They were beautiful, fragile, and
moving together, happily, inside a peace.
As I drove away, they became distant, and then,
only a glimpse, finally left their memory, alone.
I thought of Thee and Me.
My soul has taken flight on occasions in playful
spontaneity, to weave into movements which
have been intense and full of meaning, but brief,
and altogether, as in this now, distant glimpses,
to fall to memory.
In this aftertime I am alone;
I think of Thee and Me.

--one of the earliest pieces written after Richard's death–
one of two years; it draws from the experience of seeing
two yellow butterflies while driving back from Mamma's
1993-1994

Elizabeth

Captured Tears

How sweet my captured tears,
withheld and stored,
to say goodbye again,
water saved,
pouring out,
olive water,
forgotten,
on still rose petals.
Baslm again lies with red,
and verses are heard,
the organ's sound grande enough for death;
the constancy of winter rain is true,
sister to olive tears on rose petals.

And So Forever?
Yes, True, Forever

My gentle and pleasant reverie,
all the more comforting
because of melodies from many strings,
was interrupted by the bell.
I arose, quickly, to see the parcel vehicle driving away.
I opened then the kitchen door and discovered my gifts,
tardy for the season's giving.
All outside was grey, but wonderfully fresh,
from the night's rainfall;
it was cold, and I could hear birds all together,
suggesting a natural countenance
of simple splendor and friendly accommodation.
I breathed in this beauty of winter
from which I had closeted myself for some days.
I thought: "This is the way of days, before spring."
And then, as if struck
by a sudden and unexpected, heavy blow,
I stumbled and wept deeply:
You are not, cannot be here,
in this promising winter splendor;
and you will not come again to our door,
with humble packages, surprises,
narratives from the day,
and dreams for us to dream.

1993 – first, early grief –

First Sorrow

A large redbird came to his grapevine today,
beautiful, and strong and vigorous;
I thought of him and the last time he sat with
his grapevine: the wheelchair, his nurse, and
his pajamas, the late September afternoon,
his ebbing strength; the contrast was too close,
too great.
He is in the grapevine: and I grieved the beautiful
creature coming to rest on it, reminding how much
was lost, before all was gone.
How sad to come to this awareness, of how great
was the loss, and was to be, and he knew;
and there was not anything to comfort me.

--this is the first sentiment I penned following Richard's
death,
in the first spring after –
summer, 1993

Elizabeth

On Occasion

On rare occasion,
in helpless, defenseless moments,
he spoke of himself as wet and sweet,
his blood become as sugared water,
flowing into infirmity and death.
And I know, too,
such occasion,
that I am soft and tired,
and that although I cover
with silk and wool,
and with winter rabbit,
my spirit within peers out
to a world that is dying,
for its vehicle of transport,
of circumstance and time,
is diminished and shadowed,
into an infirmity of engagement;
firmness of touch and embrace,
lost, patient darkness,
growing, unto death.

Beautiful words and sounds in the noon hours
find a remembered March cold,
being out with too little sleeve,
quickly into familiar rooms,
to count treasures.
Leaves in lost cinnamon and bronze
bring in some of the conclusion of winter
as they pass with the wind among old,
tasted apartments,
leaving a grey to the sunlight of the day,
so that we were restless in these hours together.
The collected cotton blush of trees
speak of green, coming,
and the plum and pear
have shown their soft, white promise.
-Senses full now,
knowing,
being in the grasp of memory;
the light is clear from his windows,
touching,
hurting,
a near surface wound from inside,
deep,
for the rapture,
the spring was lost,
and mourned in unhappy years,
viewed from a distance.
And now,
that distance is come into me,
with lost rapture,
lost spring.

Summer Meditation

Superior, studied effort
brought the generous integrity of yesterday's songs,
touching with strength,
bringing tears,
a brief, decorated grieving for lost summer,
summer resting within a wash,
a net of warm gardenia,
fluid petals and fragrance hanging about,
a silkened, ivory breathing;
I moved within the fancy,
the truth of straight lines
in soft rose and finishing sunlight gold,
suggesting my summer body;
and in them I did not hear the summer passing,
the gardenia settling into its quieting,
moving paths into place
that have brought yesterday.
And now, today's sudden, summer tears:
meditation sweet,
your visit must call
with patience and brevity,
and infrequently,
for my heart is opened by yesterday and memory,
and the cleaving is into beauty
that I can bear
only as the intense glance of the summer lily,
or the mourning narrative
of the violin's prescribed voice.

Somehow,
in my indifference,
I learned to love you,
in the desperate hours
fringing my struggle to find wholeness.
Tardy smiles and ivory silences
came to include you,
and to know your first constancy.
-So much a sorrow
that in the indolent blossoming of my flower,
yours fared weary, with questionings,
so that unsure hands
and a faltering resolve became my gift of you.
My innocent unfairnesses,
the unseen pain
darkened our troth,
it becoming a troubled reversal
that left me with giving that could not fill,
and golden wounds
that yet cast about a winter's glow.

Cinderella's Sepulcher

When you came to me,
and offered my spirit refreshment,
my body, given my soul's empowerment,
accepted your touch and caress.
Our hearts sought each other out,
and when our houses touched,
they sang together in recognition.
And familiarity brought a continued newness,
an expectancy and joy.
I came to need your spirit of the morning,
the nightly delicacies,
so that in your absence
there is, in my deepest self,
a grave wanting,
save the memory
of the freshly unique wholeness
that so colored our mergence.
And so, I wish a sepulcher,
with repository,
where I may bring and place
the conversations and the physical touches,
the impressions and reflections
that were ours together,
that an aura may rise over the sepulcher
to lift up and find you,
for the chronicle of our hearts
can only echo
that I become daily a desert
whose only nourishment is memory.

If my Cinderella remembrances,
these small reminders throughout the day,
moments revisited-
if these could reach you,
and you not feel them vapid mortality,
perhaps memory
could be accompanied by other refreshment:
a reverie, a fancy, into the night, a dream smile,
a spring smile, a touch across.

Wretched that I am,
I yet require the corporeal for comfort,
color and shape,
form and timber.
I know that as you diminish in these old patterns,
your lights will grow more intense, more caring,
however small.
Grant that I can loose my clasp
on what is memory,
and entertain in joy your lighted spirits,
stars providing comfort to my mourning heart.
Perhaps in such a reunion,
the great distance that is between us,
our separateness,
our selves,
can, in our long denouements,
somehow in the will of each of us
for a oneness,
allow once lovely, and now kindred spirits,
one family.
It may be that in order
that we might open and enter
the chambers of our hearts,
the corporeal must waste and be thrown apart.
What is so grievous is not so much the departing,
but the partial man we become
after we say goodbye,
to prepare to follow where these have flown.
We are dragged along,
as an unseated rider,
kept from holding to his quest,

by all those things mortal.
Indeed the nature of our going draws color
in proportion to how much we hold to
and are in communication with the shadow;
our corporeal selves.
Once unfettered,
the color drawn away, the spirit full,
we can then recognize,
we can embrace
the immeasurable beauty of the soul.

Elusive Wanderer

In this birth, sleep is a wanderer,
and my lines have become tonight
as a busy road map.
In the long sighing darkness,
you were so close that I awoke
to the sensation of your body lining mine,
so that your heart lay against me,
your arms about me,
and I knew your rare, tender words.
With full wakefulness
I wished to push with great force and scream,
to understand the cathedral colors I saw.
Our body smells
had been like the summer-warmed earth
reaching up to the generous rainfall.
This thought, this loss-
and a spontaneous moan left me,
audible and telling.
Shapes appeared,
circular and pear, and undefined spaces;
sleep finally was the breath
between peaceful sounds
and I was pulled into the day

with this image salad,
struggling with memory and pain.
The fever is softened
and I am left in its quietness;
I open my hand to nothing, except every sound,
each image and color which compose my world
and which in its allness,
its completeness
is a retelling of my grief.

The Arrangement

Impressions gather, an atmosphere evolves,
and I have fancied
that you pinned violets to my fur.
They were precious with your smile
in their background.
To complete were your wonderful silences,
juxtaposing with verses of soft beauty.
There are other gifts,
those of medieval color,
sweet incense, and psalms and prayers;
more, yet, exquisite metaphors and truths,
the sun hanging late in the summer sky,
grandly round, and flame.
As the sunlight, so generous,
but of its own arrangement:
and so, so generous,
but so rare the invitation to ask,
to show the need of the shy butterfly
who wishes to be touched.

Reverent Fancy

Careful seeing finds at the heart of darkness, disbelief,
and so when I bow, you are there;
summer gardenias are fragrant,
the strawberry is full,
and we again joust with curry.
But you cannot stay,
for belief wavers;
belief is rising in darkness,
and celebrating the covenant when there is no rain;
it is holding hands that cannot be reached,
and filling up the heart with one side of feeling;
whatever patterns we draw,
belief is that we allow ourselves
which comforts and strengthens.
We may be suitor to dragons or lambs,
but we provide for our spirits
and find difficult those beings and forms
that have sprung from our reason only.
And so, you are left to wander until my heart can,
with clear arrangement,
take memory and give it life,
in regions decorated with fancy and promise.

Darkened Signature

For the first time in two years, tonight,
I have ordered Christmas cards,
a drawing of an angel,
in browntones, with a trumpet.
How strange, how sad, that I am doing
so, only to sign them with my
name alone.

Richard was with me when I last
ordered holiday cards;
now, he is gone away,
for almost two years. I miss him
tonight, in many ways,
but most, I think in his gentleness,
his quietness,
and our wonderful conversations.
It may be that the most precious
gift a man can give a woman
is his gentleness;
his strength is there already,
in the reality of the relationship.
But the gentleness stretches him,
shapes him,
and strengthens the relationship.
All of the clamor of rising and retiring

and everything that is in
between,
and finally the closing,
do not in any way diminish
this exquisite thing
of beauty.

Elizabeth
1994

Widening

Agatha, Moi

Of a moment, I imagined that I have spoken,
about many things to others,
and when they stand by and look into my face,
I ask if I have spoken ought that I should not,
yet, in innocence's knowings, unacceptably.
And then, in my fancy, they respond,
"Oh no... it is only that we have not often
listened to the saying of so much right and good."
And then I sigh, with a pleased relief,
that I have loosed what I could not contain,
and I have pleased...I have found the center,
I have heard the true melody...and stars dress my
person.
I have spoken true...and I have pleased...and stars
dress me.
I will not reach for the sun and moon.

Of Harold and Agatha
My dualistic feelings of responsibility – "thine ownself"

Dragon Tears

I could not sleep, and I could not be awake.
And so I drifted somewhere
between the forever in darkness and the moment that
is now.
You are with me again, and you are slipping painfully
away again.
My heart is a heavy staccato,
and my fingertips weep, comrades to my brimming
eyes.
The horns wound my heart, and then the melody is
finished.
Chariots with their fire have told me once more what I
carefully know:
that we were together, but now are only bittersweet
whispers
for whom compassionate angels, with rehearsed
petitions,
graciously soften the darkness and gather devotional
starlight
that we might have our desperate and fragile touch.
How bitter the dragon's tears; so much a Samaritan,
the smoke which can dim the eye.

I cannot reference today, 11-15-2002, the
significance of "dragon tears", but from the
content of this early verse, its subject and
tone, I must have had, from some source, idea
to their bittersweetness, perhaps, because of its
early characteristics, reference to loss of
Richard.

Tenuous Rhythm

When our spark ignited, it flamed out,
and ate up all of the darkness in our worlds.
We were explorers of deepest soul, and softest touch,
and gave with a great generosity to the needs of each
other.
But we soon learned that our generosities were
covered,
at unhappy times, by dark, blanketing clouds,
followed by begging in our need,
accompanied by tortuous and angry words.
In time, the clouds would lift, and there would be the
fresh of dew,
the abiding manna.
And we would enjoy flowers and sunshine once again.
On a day, the cloud settled on me, so that I could not
offer at all to him,
and he was alone.
He left briefly, while I dressed, to go across the way to
his rooms;
he was away some time, and then returned.
In the evening he recounted the activity of his absence.
He has positioned himself on his bedroom floor,
his toe to discharge his weapon… and considered.
With an accusing realization I knew my darkness had
wounded him.
And then into the years my darkness wounded him
still, by being lifted.
But we did not ever break the rhythm.

There were many clouds for both of us and many
flowers and sunshine.
On that day, I had given attention to dressing, more
particularly to my darkness.
He had enjoyed sport with ideas of life and love and
death.
But he came back to me... to come to prefer me with
my darkness.
And so, with either, I had the quality I required.
I could not help, though, to raise each day a question,
and sometimes, I was surprised with my answer.

Of mine and Richard's
troubled courtship

Second Fire

In this season
which commemorates our discovering each other,
the pledging of our vows,
of the dark that crept in
and began the great darkness and separation,
I struggle to remember,
with a measure of despair, still.
If I could have known, then, how precious,
how without measure those moments were,
and with what deep sentiment
they would be remembered,
I should have declared a great silence,
that record be made
of their singular beauty,
this time of love and promise,
and then of loss.
Unhappily, the reality of now is close,
too complete,
for you are not in it,
not to come, not to touch, not to be,
and your chair has been removed.
And so, we mourn love as forever as it is absent,
walking a silent sequel,
drawing light from the first fire.

Elizabeth, early years after Richard's death

Devotional

With the devotion of a servant,
I have honored you;
and with the excitement,
the joy of the great December mass of Christ,
I have anticipated your smile;
but you are removed, maintenant,
within the vast and distant chamber
buttressed by the brilliant gold of the early sun,
and the quiet, full flower of the sunset's fragile
moment.
Yet the aloneness of midnight
speaks a soliloquy of our separation,
and my wretchedness.
Today in nature has been flawless,
my universe of senses and spirit, complete;
the sun is now withdrawing,
leaving enchantment in the shadows,
suggestive, promising of the dark monastery of night.
And when the music is torturously beautiful,
I not only mourn your presence now,
but the youth we knew between us.

Unrighteous Refection

*There was a bliss, but only in the inner seam of the
wretchedness.*
I bowed away from other loves to be yours alone,
and you devoured me, complete,
the me you fashioned, on the dish you chose,
without a thought of my replenishment.
I willingly fell to your ravishing, but understanding
with difficulty the disquietude,
the strange stances I found to please you.
If you had raised fine silver to carve my heart,
with royal condiments to the side,
yours would have been an elegant, generous feast,
but when done, my mystique known,
I should have still been without, a nothing,
not lingering deep, red garnet drops
*but blood pale, remembering only faintly passion and
life.*
*When you were satisfied that I no longer had essence
to spoil,*
you threw away the crumbs and pieces,
*and I lie here, crumbs and pieces, weeping that I am
now*
neither nourishment to you or a soul in myself.
*All that is left is my pale blood that tints the liner of
the castaway.*

Of Richard, again.

The Smile

In the full of it rested established peace;
in its mysterious contours lay the wings over my
embers;
in its strength spread forth, deep, my foundation,
and in the fading
was fashioned my threadbare furnishings.
Its mercurial wiseness caught me always begging,
accepting as of raw meat to a lesser creature.
And so, I walked in parade,
and sat on the orange stoo1,
and in moments rare,
I stood upright
and was accepted in all appropriateness.

Richard, the me he allowed,
for a great, long while,
about twenty years-

In Confusion

We are two in confusion,
like an egg shaken,
here, and removed, in every shadow,
away, away:
loving, hating, giving and drawing apart.
-And now hands across to you,
still bent from your blows;
and you, searching for my face,
out of days of struggle for a place away from me,
now become your hero and husbandwoman;
with the counsel of memory,
I have, in all, known no greater statue,
but there is, in this recognition, yet today
a sorrow still.

Still today, November 12, 2002;
I do not know why such had to be.
Elizabeth

The Rebuke

Neither lineage nor estate,
war with strangers,
or brother upon brother;
not son unto mother or irreverence
and refusal of the cup-
none touched me so as that circumstance that he loved
me,
unto tomorrow;
and that slowly and quickly he did not love me,
as in those first, those three exquisite years.
His dying love was itself a circumstance,
and so, he did not again love with his first heart;
unto reason then, the gravest circumstance was that I
lost his love;
after giving so that I cannot forget, he took it again
unto himself,
darkly, to wager and tease, whispering yesterdays,
finally, in scorn,
put me aside until the last hour.
The suffering of this circumstance rebukes all others.

Bloodspill

I came to clean dust
from books resting on our bedside table,
and innocently picked up the cord to the lamp;
with a long consideration,
I wept a sigh,
heavy and weary;
I lifted the cord to see residual, spilled drink,
dried now some years.
The wine appeared,
in the seam of the cord, as dried blood.
Then, like bringing a great light
to an unfortunate sack of rats,
my thoughts scattered in all directions,
pulling in the dark of corners and sad shadows.
More, were distracting thoughts
as with the arrival of a visiting child,
who when striking the piano keys
in awkward and unknowing patterns,
allows, altogether, a harsh and sharp staccato.
Conclusions, thus,
persuaded my heart to speak,
that I viewed the residue as my blood,
and so, I speak of it-
blood spilled in futile efforts at wholeness.
It was he who spilled the red wine,
but in that unhappy movement,
he spilled me out, so,
in many troubled hours.
He spilled me out and down,

and only in the closing,
when he acted out of an humble gratitude,
was I somewhat replenished and lifted.
And now that the everyday,
placed and necessary
tasks have been discharged,
I feel a deep grief once again.

When the waters...

When the waters were filled with daisies,
why did you not bring just one;
was it that you were unable to see the daisies
or that you did not understand
how much I cherished their simple loveliness.
And so speak your smile,
and the wearing of your band,
treasures all, withheld
and therefore establishing forever in my heart
their absence of white and gold,
empty of flesh and honor.

Again, of Richard, unhappily –
flowers – not brought –
his wedding band – not worn

Dark Peace

-And so,
in the years of silence,
when my heart could not sing,
there came a learned discipline
of thought and mood,
of the measure of effort to task;
my fancies grew,
billowing up from a house of grey
into marvelous colors of flowers,
their sculpted, petaled lips
speaking soft verses, soft melodies.
Came then, a visitation, a peace,
out of my longings,
that in their denial,
their unfulfilling,
lay reprieve to my struggle.

I did not write, could not compose for about twenty years,
those so difficult with Richard; I did not return to writing
until after his death, but more certainly in my long
convalescence following the accident that very nearly
required my leg.

His words sped like arrows,
with grave intention,
to my defenseless heart;
and I knew wisdom
to be on the other side of the innocence.
That I have lost to love
does not allow one to accept his soothing of my bruised
vessel
and yet that he housed need to,
likewise, be comforted.
When his eyes closed,
will he see my form;
ah, yes,
but only suggestive covering of another's heart.
In all innocence
my love to him is furnished by past lessons,
and to me his wisdom should not grant this maneuver
so that we can only fancy
that we share intentions of surface lights,
love that has sprung up, intensely, in the hour, that
there is no memory, no shadows.
Images dressed in shrouds
and the grey net of memory cause wounds
not touched by grace;
and to place them in another is cunning
almost beyond truth,
yielding a masquerade macabre.
And so wisdom laughs,
and we know
that just as darkness companions to quiet,
wisdom is near to pain.

We Together

And I knew both love and anger,
within a triangle,
lightly colored of the orange fruit;
could the sacred Three
with that I know
bittersweetness fully complete,
hours filled with light out of dark;
will my fullness hold long moments,
empty and grey,
and know sunshine
standing no more than the head of shadow.
Autumn smiles,
forming lips of gold,
to kiss with a quiet beauty,
wandering,
carrying a woman's grace,
into winter and communion stillness.
The glory in chrismation begs humility,
knowing enough
suddenly becoming a poor verse of apostasy.
And so,
I will take the hand of him to my side,
for we together see the triangle.

Each token, when first rediscovered,
tears out the heart,
and it lies trembling,
a tender wound, and
tears can only suggest how memory touches the soul.
I will weep, alone of tears,
and say of it to no one,
but take into myself the value of each token
to be stirred toward you and our hours together.
Indeed, I will place the tokens,
once favored,
in a dark place,
that in some beautiful night, yet,
to bring them out, each alone,
to know in weeping,
that you are with me still.
I cannot bear the truth I know,
that with you now there is a great sameness,
should I not touch a forgotten token
to be remembered again.
Sameness is a curse of acceptance,
and within it we cannot know recognition.
And so I will, with resolve,
enjoy again the pain of the covered fire in memory.

Nourishment of Ashes

Words out of vaporous smoke,
footsteps pressed by the scarlet in fire,
standing, lifting out of volcanic chairs,
their cushions smiling,
flame and blue, haloed white-
so that you touch me,
and I am covered by angry rain,
you, who pulls my fire to satisfy your coals,
and I who burn in this nourishing
so that ashes fall into my finishing,
their glory to fly into the distance
too far to see.

2000 and I

I have heard again
the magnificent sounds of master Struass,
used to depict the moment
when insight and circumstance
happily meet and embrace,
giving us the concept of instruments,
to help in the long journey we then began.
The music teased my memory
so that I at last responded.
There was another spring which hosted these sounds,
and when the sounds were at their zenith,
you lifted me up to your face and shoulder,
supported by a wonderful smile
and you pressed me to you.
There were smiles, and happiness,
for the arrangement you required was in place;
you had strength and I was dependent.
Unhappily, you did not dress your lamps well,
for thieves broke through,
unaddressed for many years,
and stole your strength,
the thieves of fear,
indecision and lack of trust, and deceit.
During summer and winter,
the battle raged,
you, losing ground, steadily,
and I ministered to your wounds.
You did not lift me now,
and we seldom smiled;

and silence became our conversation.
And then, with the years,
the moment came,
when in your weakness, your strength returned,
and you met death valiantly
and my ministrations paled in your glory.
The thieves were careless;
they overlooked your resolve,
which carried you up in peaceful vapors,
leaving me
with lonely acceptance and deep admiration.

I cannot be weary,
for it is at times,
imprudent, to allow fatigue.
My burden is not a bag of stones,
darkening my shoulders,
but rather is a pensive weight present everywhere,
everywhere that memory can gain entrance.
I must whisper it away into a pleasant darkness,
or perhaps,
into a lighted bliss of smiles.
When we entertain our memories,
they leave us, together,
fragile and empowered,
with truth and suggestion.
The harvest of cranberry
and the royalty in red and gold
promise warmth and offer invitation to walk again
the sentiments that must bind together
our reaching, but mummers' souls.
There can be a sacredness in darkness,
but we can, yet, be sometimes foolish
in answering the thousand eyes
of the darkness in memory.
Whispered woodhue, handsome wine, lighted;
sun gold and red straw,
companioned to smiles;
scarlet, passionate scarlet;
sweet basil;
together at table;
and tears, the nectar in good-bye:
In a beautiful, quiet frenzy,

so visit me, all;
cover me and let me breathe
the gentleness of the nightshade mandrake,
to enjoy the intoxication of a dreamer's knowing,
to be furnished the cranberry
and the red and gold,
alone of the bag of stones.

Violet Crescendo

Feelings gather and speak,
in the difficult moments before mid-day;
they compose a continuous grey,
and are filled with blue, mosaic afterthoughts.
I am rather the child who cannot leave her tender self
and move to a larger, more resilient whole.
I rise, fatigued, still, from responsibility and caring;
the sunlight's generous glory is slighted by my peevish
child,
and so is without full recognition and appreciation.
Grief from lost loves and their painful leavetakings
clothe me,
instead, darkly, so that I walk slowly,
burdened as a weighted shadow and sighs out of
midnight;
I am sustained by these, my tired dreams, and the
stained lily,
fushsia's tenuous introduction to deep violet;
yet, an apologetic catching of a past fragrance,
and a portion of a walk interrupted
and closed off when I wanted yet to touch.
I am alone, where we are when the evening falls hard
on us;
I am in a darkened crescendo, alone,
its zenith, my acknowledged heartache,
and a desperate sorrow its conclusion.

Often and again,
I place us together;
on some occasions we hold musical instruments,
and in other times we gather flowers;
-And warm still is the shared cup;
but the thought,
the dream of moon-spoken daffodils,
the daytime image,
these are interrupted:
a curtain of darkness,
a fall of great waters,
a grey fog that clouds
so that I know the seduction of death:
these come but move away
and the golden circle is not then closed,
and I am alone.
All is, for a space, a shadowed recollection,
but then, as the years have held in place,
the images return,
to offer joy,
a knowing of oneness,
closeness such that a blossom hangs between us,
no matter that the golden circle is not yet closed.

Not Yet

I almost let it fall away today:
the sorrow, the regret and fatigue,
some small portions of anger and resentment.
I did almost let it fall;
I felt winds of freedom,
freedom to self-pacing,
to exuberance, spontaneity.
In a space too small to measure,
I wished to let it fall.
And then, like a heavy rope
that might have raised a curtain,
I saw the stage;
I recognized all the burdens you were, you are;
with them I have you,
with these bags of grief and darkness,
moving around, side to side.
As the blackness in midnight,
you are in our darkness.
To let the baggage go, and be free:
the turn is that without you,
I should be newly enslaved to my emptiness,
and you would be unable to comfort me,
the game put aside.
And so, I did not let it fall away today.

Bittersweet Window

The window to my improvised bedroom is very friendly
to me.
It offers the first light of day, the conclusion to night
and struggle.
It inspires courage and hope, a spirit toward effort,
leaving behind what now are only grey, unhappy
images.
For in the darkness, my fears come to me,
attended by tasks undone and promises not kept.
I know anew the heaviness, the burden of my body.
My beloved companions are brought to me again,
in conversation I do not hear, but I know their words.
And although I know the light suggests hope and the
good must always to come,
the darkness suggests a finishing, a conclusion.
Light and dark, the sun and moon, clarity and shadow;
ascribed presentations of good and evil, always
together, interminably.
What am I to know?
That it is merely a playing with, more a jousting with
light,
that we think we can know happiness?

The Answer

I slept,
my head on Jacob's pillow of Bethel rock;
and came to me his angels,
ascending and descending the ladder
into and away from heaven,
concurrently into awakening,
but there was not a blessed quiet,
for all about,
in the open expanse of thought,
in the avenues carrying memory and sentiment,
sounded a cry,
a questioning, pleading an answer:
"It was true, it was whole; can it be,
to soothe me in eternity's boundless space?"
The voice rang,
of chestnut and olive,
searching a peace on the other side of knowing;
and so, into yesterday,
light and shadow, words and silences,
gifts and slights found review,
these cataloguing
alongside my ascending and descending;
with grief and remembered joy, as the last ascending,
appeared the face of love,
speaking,
with instruction to look into my separate heart,
that sealed to hurt and loss.
Opening, then, the boxes
within found small tins of olive hours,

rounds of chestnut days,
olive gardenia in chestnut warmth,
with pause,
and touching a tenderness of groomed of death.
And then,
with careful, concluding steps onto the stone pillow,
an answer sang to the force of voice:
"It was true, it was whole."

And coming to the still,
awareness held in pocket, with careful hand,
first joy blossomed into the magic of clean selfhood,
with confidence and true bearing.
The metaphysical obscure lay close beside,
the paradox of the binding
and freedom of truth given tolerable distance.
The sun in coming excellence,
the dark in its motionless quiet,
covering all into refuge-
these took thought
and led it toward the innocence in the new day.
Yearnings, urgings, libidinal frolic
reaching foreboden boundaries, these together
brought full consciousness and the fall of will.
And so,
the day advanced into growing joy, as the hour to ripe fruit,
contained in a golden cup of reason
whose bags of sandwords came,
with hidden ease, to taint the joy,
allowing, in the binding up,
only struggle and slow continuing.
His dark crown with chestnut lights
gave over to the bend of my arm, brought lovingly,
comfortingly, to my breast,
his chestnut receedings of careful drawing;
the day bears hard,
coming suddenly into its shadow
with the hurt of love's recollection,
holding for a long moment,
without breathing,
precious capture in the passing breath of pain.

The Wall

Deep, red garnet stones and promises
near Valentine's Day,
all mixed with scornful words
and looks of complete contempt
at my "feigned" weakness;
–a slight kiss for my warm cheek,
followed by reproaches and sharp
instructions —
long hours of painful silence
conclude with a quick, dutiful
embrace,
and then obscenities.

Am I too sensitive? But that is where
I meet the wall;
The "sensitive I" is me.
And so – how am I to care.

Again

Today had been Easter Sunday,
and, innocently enough,
I let it leave me still
more alone.
"Bring some honeysuckle from
behind the fence" –
"Why?"
"Because it so smells like Easter" –
"Oh, I didn't know Easter
smelled".

Again, I faced the wall.

Elizabeth
early 1970's

The Dreamer

And the dreamer saw two figures,
who, in shadow,
kept two birds, unclothed,
in company with a plant,
handsome and great,
one which surged upward,
its markings like an intense latticework,
dark,
having a heavy fragrance.
Their love was alive forever,
convoluted and perverse,
without the gentle gifts of reciprocity,
latitude and distance.
They lived thus,
into the night,
and no one knew,
no one saw,
no one,
save one of the two,
left now to thought and example,
and to dreams.

The secret, of mine, with Richard,
as it became.

Full Song

In Florence

Per favore
quando potrei
compare acqua

Forgotten words, of forgotten hours,
offered in innocence,
smiling innocently still;
now found,
there is only the warmth of the melted ice,
and from the fallen petals of the rose
lifts a distant fragrance
that is yet of its first composition.
You are a shadowed standing,
being out of your plenished whole:
a knowing of memory and recognition,
the embroidered silk of feeling,
the glow of days within.

In Europe together

Oh my soul,
harbor to my thought,
be quiet, let me swan walk, let me sleep.
I do not wish anymore their voices,
images of youth,
they in their gold.
Let a great nothingness fill my ears,
for all the melodies I hear
cast a bittersweet timbre,
and a quiet silence
would furnish vanilla to dark cadences.
A circumstance of meeting,
an arrangement of summer flowers,
rainfall in sunshine and the shadows
of laughing children embracing each other,
these become a richly embroidered, fragrant memory.
This memory encompasses fresh cologne,
darkening gardenias,
and warm, wet sand in a friendly ditch.
Can we truly know peace
when part of our heart is taken away,
and part is left with us.
The moments all gathered together,
as gently as we might,
are a forever through which
the broken whole reaches for its lost part.

Grief Entertained

There was a time that I remembered
the summer hours together,
the energy between us,
and I remember the smell of his body, close.
And I remember remembering
but time has taken the deep sentiment
and left the drawn particulars.
I do not anymore look
to find an ambiance with his body.

A melody, a memory, and again grief;
the hour suddenly grows dark.
Grief is a living thing
and dies only to time.
In the betweenwhile there is just to weep,
to make suitable goodbyes,
and with a conscious will,
speak of the day without the dragon in it;
for when we appropriately pretend,
time passes
and we have killed a portion of the dragon
we did not see.
The guest who is not entertained, will,
without ceremony,
leave the banquet.

An arrangement of thought to deal with all of the losses between
Dr. Sutton's death and my leg, though, beginning with specific
reference to Richard –

The Healing Pain

Oh my dear, my own brave heart,
I have suddenly remembered, as true,
your strength when you held me, while I trembled,
wrapping me about
with your ample but careful hands;
more, I have again a glimpse
of the quiet kindness in your eyes,
a deep chestnut love,
as I faced you and wept.
And so, with your hands and eyes
you once covered me with healing.
I can only imagine that you felt the strength
and understanding you gave away.
With these, your gifts,
I came to stand alone, and without you.
Now with this sudden remembrance
I wish and hope that you knew then your strength,
and trusted it to me,
that you knew in it honor and confidence,
and felt perhaps that you, on occasion,
walked in robes of purple and gold.
I know a deep anguish in these moments,
for I still tremble and weep
during the quietness of night,

and I need your strength and gentleness,
not so much to stand, but to feel, with your touch,
a wish to stand.
It is out deeply crimsoned center
that we first know loss,
and it is in this innermost portion
that we must begin to know healing.
In conversations and prayers you are close to me;
in the quieting of the light
and unfolding of the bed,
you are nearby;
and in the cold water of morning
and the first opening of the lock,
you are with me still.
In these moments,
a sad procession yielding a concert of feeling,
I must know you are with me,
but I must lose, somehow,
the pain that you are real to me,
but only as a figure and touch
that can be drawn by words.
The realization of your presence, in pain,
I must exchange for your presence at a distance,
which will, if less,
be more without the coloring of your absence.
Natural inclinations do not allow

my heart to live in fancy or in shadow.
In you I know my greatest loss,
and so, of you
will be my greatest effort toward wholeness.
It is almost a poetic sadness
that this healing will allow my greatest pain.

In the late afternoon, when flowers again
dressed, seasonally, your rest,
you, my three loves,
the sun did not find heavy clouds, in the first
roads, as he had not on entering them,
they, then, the return roads,
except as his apology around their outer
parameters, lighted gause casements
bordering floating, dark melodies,
fatigued grey tulle
which wished to hang;
but with my thoughts gathering, accessing the
interstate from Martinsville, surely in a
final constancy, came again running
from the beautiful June day given over
to the caring husbandman
joining his handwork, his only
recent thoughtful touch; reaching
forward found the image of rain of
thirty-seven days,
wishing a forgetfulness of the reminding
anniversary, the rain to fall
again on remembered red and balsm
fur.
--And then lighted from the west, the brilliant eye
found vanishing white giving up
summertime blue, polar bears,
perhaps, looking back to small,
drifting ice,
or supposed islands wandering,
as England's drawing in centuries

too far distant to mourn her losing
present.
--With an almost wishfulness, under the lock of
another distance, it seems, in my
innermost, my knowing
the all of it, but feeling the none
of it.

The room was found almost dark, the balcony
made more lovely with contrasting, falling
moonlight, onto cold chairs, and
plants lying in the dark impotence of frostbite.
I did not hear music, or see apples, but their
images found in my thought, and I did
not wish the lamp,
but to let silence employ association,
to couple their marriage with
memory, and with the net of the
mystique that such
beauties can drape and know,
to hold again the generous lovely,
a spirituality that weeps over its only night
hour, and positions about, among afternoon clouds,
day stars of
pardon, under whom thoughts,
which had gathered in their near, recent, soon
presence,
could not find their fraternity without
sentiments dressed with mourning's
select, yet rarest beauty.

Driving to Wesson, visiting the cemetery
to put out winter flowers, and driving
home again;
and later, on going up to bed, with no
light, finding moonlight pouring
onto the balcony,
knowing again the sweet pain in memory,
to chide my heart, for its
moments with it.

December 28, 2001

Standstill

The day has completed its turn,
and the light has gone away;
I stand alone, without purpose or conversation;
I am at a standstill;
all have fare and I have none.
Melodies chide me,
and once beautiful words
seem an empty cup of sentiment.
Where is all that makes the day,
in whose absence the night is left, alone.
Camellias and early daffodils
are cold and ashen,
for the crown of smiles
has slipped into a quiet majesty
that prepares for tomorrow.
I am at a standstill;
perhaps, properly, I should be crumpled
like today's handkerchief,
or the receipt from the grocery,
to be thrown into the wash and wastebasket.
For being used and wrinkled
do not credential us to sit in prepared light,
in the presence of daisies out of season.

Bright daisies in Autumn,
for a number of years
kept for Richard, for they
were the last, remaining
image he could see, other than
my hair,
at his death.

The Program

My mirrors reflect the nearly finished day;
I move, shadow-like, through my rooms
and yesterday's quieted laughter
is almost a reproach.
I cannot add more than a lamp
to the vast outer darkness,
even that which is in fences,
and so travelers must somehow find their way;
more, my wisdom is as presumptuous water
thrown into the daytime sky,
and my steps are as vapor already lifted up,
their record only as my breath.
My tendernesses are like color
taken into the veins of glorious blossoms,
to their petals, already in fading hues.
And my love is like a distant, haunting melody,
struggling on the ground with its broken wing.

The Fancy

Fine horses in green pasture,
kingly strength flowing,
their silent neighs
recording a new spring of their happy lineage;
dogwood beside, finding its flowering
in sunlight
that lavishes its full presence on the waiting day:
hungry eyes glean,
and in their harvest
find a sorrowful wisdom
dressing the season of first beauty,
but with an aside of joyful knowing to reach,
even with awkward, foolish touch,
that this time be sounded,
its voice captured in its ringing,
inside eyes that see beyond the pasture,
or sun-visited flowers;
into the wealth of consummated pleasure,
its resting,
the wealth that lies in the soft, grey flesh of memory
which bears all gifts,
all wisdom into acceptance,

into a hope that in coming hours,
those into darkness,
within the riddle,
be found as true
the fancy that a spiritual flesh burns with beauty,
without smoke or ash,
but again into itself,
a radiance aware,
perpetual.

Judgement Aperitif

Oh Olive,
your Rose loses breath;
dream to me,
allow to me a glimpse
that can bridge the space
between knowledge and infinity,
and fire my heart with the sun
that empowers love's faithful troth.
Show me in a smile
that death contracts to be
but a deeply drunk, judgement
aperitif provided to the banquet of oneness.
Do not pass away
until I see light touch your chestnut hair,
until your hands frame my face;
indeed nothing more,
for your voice is known at first consciousness,
and with the last image of day.

A Rare Edelwiss

Yesterday I placed fresh, yellow daisies
on the bunching tables.
I can see them:
I have just looked at them,
with all of their wonderful, sunlit brilliance.
You did see others of them,
and then you could not see them,
except as a lovely,
wished-for impression of yellow.
I place them here always
so that now that you can see,
you will see them always:
fresh, beautiful, yellow and with life
a happy arrangement of my love.

Yellow daisies for Richard,
after his death, kept
fresh, five years or so –

This Shortened Path

If I held still the pendulum,
so that there would be no hour sounded;
if I draped all of the glass
so that there would shine no sun or moon;
if I put away sad love songs,
and if I did not begin the day with his name,
could the distance between our last good-bye
and today's absence be lessened.
And if he should not find pleasure
in this shortened path,
I would go into a wood
and let free away a dove,
that it might bear him to lighted splendor,
and he would be filled, and return again to me.
Into this homecoming
would fall golden and jeweled confetti,
and musical balloons would rise
in their grande finale,
a brilliant burst of royal purple,
and rose-stained honeysuckle.
And soft whispers with chapel bells
will offer their joyful salutations.

-Of Richard

Buttons

The paw of a sled dog,
no longer soft pink,
but sand-colored within black,
and crusted to smoothness;
foretold of snow,
the creature was stationed to walk,
in his lineage fur,
on piercing warm clay and sand, and straw;
still, ever answering.

A bluish purple wound in the oval of his right thumb,
it was long in healing,
long, eternal, bleeding through into the folded hands,
respectfully placed in the coffin;
deep purple, reverent wisdom.

Desperately seeking out light enough to draw,
grave, pulsating hope struggled,
hope that the centimeter found,
that faith would allow,
might be correct;
not asking or refusing the execution.

Charms to carry,
dressed inside my silver,
pouring from my fingertips,
guiding my steps in the path;

these are sentiments,
buttons of communion resolve,
taken again and again,
and strength worn,
like used leather
so that they are fashioned just now to hold me,
one side to the other.

Love's Exultation

Evening hours and a long song's tender words
fall upon my rooms,
companioning to my aloneness,
which rises to speak to them;
the suggestion of tears falls impotent
that they measure the loss
mirrowed in these presences.
You have left empty these my rooms
and cannot enter again.
Your absence is like a grave wound
whose issue is greater
and more crimsoned in these hours.
Do souls lift into the heavens,
becoming formed light,
with golden and other trappings regal;
or does the soul find its own glory,
its individual, lighted place.
Perhaps, then, you might be found in a quiet grotto.
Where psalms could be read;
yet in a grande tower with expanses of glass
and rooms that permit the enjoyment of fine tobacco;
still it may be that heaven could be found
in an humble hut, of awkward thatch,
suitable for ever increasing prayers.
But finding you
would only give direction of my meditations;
indeed, altogether, they present, in urgency,
the pregnant telling of my wish for your content.
And so, I offer petitions that your sighs

be as the closing of angel wings;
that your rising up be fashioned
after the water's first embrace of the sun;
that your cup collect the color of the ripe
pomegranate,
its bouquet suggesting
the lifting of wild plums out of their earthtones;
and to comfort in the hours lost to we two,
I wish for you the amusement
in the unpredictable dancing light of angelic fireflies.
A terrestrial exchange has been redeemed
by the imbuing of a complexion celestial;
that begun with an humbled hope,
and faint understanding has become love's exultation.
In the petition was found a sweet savor,
acceptable in its love's completeness.
And so, I know; I have touched you,
for I have found again, your smile.

Conclusion

The time was after the storm,
and the moon shown forth;
there was a full orchestration of grey and light,
yet a soft glow,
like a gathering of ivory satin
brushed with dark fern,
and without lay a quiet stillness
that sang nature's sovereignty.
In these moments
I fancied that my heard did not beat,
and I quickly reviewed my loss.
Would my praise to the jeweled butterfly,
touching about the spider's night embroidery,
no longer be raised;
would I forfeit the words
from the golden treasury of morning songbirds;
and would my glance
not anymore fall on the diamonds of dew
as they laughingly climb the sun's rays into heaven.
At different junctures, we take our heart
I took my heart and held it in my hand;
in its quiet lay conversation with you,
and I wept with the thought.
And so, I took my heart to a chapel to pray,
that flowers and arched moonlight
offer me conclusion.
Into our hand and decide to walk the distance
or give in to the despair of loss, what ever its
fashioning,
in the beating of my heart is my knowing

so that I cleave to my songbirds and sunlight,
and so I will wait unto the feast is complete
to then enter into a dialogue of reunion,
two wayfarers that walk the same path.

Elizabeth

Refusing the Evening Star

I have, in moments too close,
stepped from the precipice
that borders on the most of grey,
a nothingness absolute,
from which the heart, in very strength, is irretrievable.
Mirrored to me was my faltering carriage in motion,
a carriage knowing without purpose;
the days then stretched out before,
filled with empty movements,
pulling their life away,
with I, alone, to find their pleasure.
In the light, noonday smiles to me,
breakfast having been of a variable hour,
the appointment finding my will;
nightfall calls out aloneness before
sighs distant of morning and yesterday, falling over
shadows into darkness.
If, indeed, I do live,
the clock alone knows my hours,
and once announced, they do not sound again.
In fear, I look,
scales on my eyes,
onto my emptiness, my aloneness,
to find a path of light and hope.
It is not yet my twilight;
the evening star speaks to me,
but I have known rapture,
and even now, it touches me.
To finish is not in this hour,
for rapture and greyness do not companion together.

Encounter

His spirit held on to the silence
and the night was perfumed by summer flowers;
her heart accepted every presence
and she knelt to pray
that they might never leave her,
in completeness,
for her heart required his spirit
in her darknesses;
and the perfume, which covered and made,
on somewise,
sweeter his lasting dark,
threw about suggestive shadows
dark, not transitory,
but quickly complete,
out of which lift dancing images,
alive, from dark flames.

Visiting Images

Visiting images, quickly passing, nearly lost,
their beauty like an unnamed fragrance,
touching,
reminding of that hidden, but, still, present,
encouraging a searching
which unveils sentiments
growing rich in their patient waiting:
the mourning of youth for beauty imagined,
the pathos of innocence lost,
establishing inevitable,
its demands ever strengthened
with increasing corporal and spiritual wisdoms-
the bed in new defilement,
war's glory,
jousting with grace;
knowing in night's dark silence
the garden's bittersweet legacy,
beautiful sorrow behind,
opening to poignant grief
whose record becomes its wealth:
worded splendor,
embellishing the ordinary
and honoring that rare, exalting effort and knowing
out of bearing and prevailing.

The Forgiven Silence

Like two splendid horses who know,
quietly,
their bearing and grace,
we walk through the days,
not sorrel or roan,
but in the ebony out of midnight,
I, terrestrial, into warmth and the golden dusk,
and in parallel fashion, you,
on the edge of heaven,
in perpetual light;
our neighing of warmest chestnut
and the blue of deepest sea
speaks our hearts across the chasm.
At the closing of my day, into the dusk,
I must pause,
and you withdraw with the sun;
I feel that you mourn me in these hours,
but celestial light comes to fill up my space,
until the sun leads you back to me, again,
and we take our sunsteps in his smile.
In the silence between our walks,
eternity shows herself to us.
But we are two forgiven
the endless silence
out of the dusk into the mornings,
for my grief honors the warm petal,

the ripened fruit,
the strength in the jointed reed;
it is not yet the sameness of light;
there is knowledge,
and the quietness has not descended.

I watched a large, handsome redbird
playing touch and away with his grapevine,
in these soft moments of the noon hour.
His plumage was attractively blended
between reds and browns,
and his mood was appropriately alert,
but unquestionably confident.
It was not apparent in flight,
but he, this redbird,
walked as though he carried a secret,
perhaps a hidden, treasured message.
The leaves of the grapevine,
beautiful in concert with all of the season's greens,
bent with his gently fondling.
All of the players, leaf, limb and flower
are wearing robes of renewal
and cannot hide their blushing promise;
there is the warm, moist soil
that nourishes his grapevine
and there are the leaves and needles,
forming splendid and reverent memorials
to the tiny seed,
of the first touch of life,
save the fertile and giving thought.
The trees do not wait for their sun's blessing,
but reach, always, upward toward it.
He is in the grapevine yet,
and so I have come, in passing by,
to pause and reflect.
Ah, Harold,
receive and delight in my tender growth,

that I, Agatha, may please thee,
Sir Harold, once again,
for though I am earthy yet,
I also rest with you in these beautiful times;
I wish that I may take with me
from these grapevine moments
the treasured message
that is in your allowing your presence to me.

On a familiar route,
I saw two large Yuka plants
with beautiful, collectively, pineapple-shaped
blossoms.
The fall season had not yet touched them.
The larger blossoms stood, tall,
out of the centers of their green and sharp leafy urns,
one on either side of a driveway.
It was startling to see such magnificent blooms,
two collections of many individual,
of such a pure white hue
and so late in the autumn season.
The tiny white flowers
clung together in exquisite innocence
with much like the fantasized, suggestive promise
of a group of chaste nuns,
pale white against their black habits,
with none of the sun's tint,
cloistered, themselves together in their cell.
So pictured is my heart,
with its promise of strongly fragile feelings,
but closeted,
where soft, intense songs and meditations
bring you to me, Harold,
and fill these gentle, still hours, to close me
to the world, open and away.

Over and Again

The chorus of good-byes
spoke out into heavy subject and hue;
a dying orchid,
in shades of grieving crimson,
made time's brown, with gold,
shown the small light of monastery services.
And so,
in warm winter winds,
over and again,
I touch my waiting hand,
and walk,
in the company of one shadow.
My passion knows only the bed of reverie,
the touch of memory and fancy;
my songs can be not any but dirges,
my flowers to hang,
each, its face,
with a grey cloth.
To offer and be refused,
to lose whatever has been granted,
to remember in silence-
these, to be then the orchid's crimson,
the monastery's small light.

The Broken Dove

Seasons,
those hours gathered and dressed,
fill up the days
with the changing familiarity of family-
these have done again the bidding
of the thoughtful and able painting master,
offering their ascribed hues,
and the warmth that finds among them
its particular companion.
The color of grey is company now,
with its attending chill.
The journey of the year reaches its closing,
and once more decorations are taken
from their patient waiting.
Surprises afforded by memory's frailty
find the day with merriment;
but, with effort, yet,
memory cannot allow passing over
the small, white porcelain dove,
bridal ivory in flight,
with no suggestion of its broken wing,
mended, as unto holding salvation.
There was the grey chill,
following an autumn
with deepest gold and early twilight;
its beauty wept in its finality.
Mourning hung over that within my rooms,
and that without, and I perished
to go beyond death's mercurial calling,

to find beauty untouched by its threatening sting;
the treasure found became the dove,
to rest upon the quiet evergreen,
hanging near the bottom of the large tree,
a new purity, a first freshness,
to only, in the desperate distance for life,
be unseated and broken.
In the long afterward,
it was found lying,
quite as it had fallen,
and with tears and care,
it was helped again to wholeness.
The coming light,
its graceful struggle;
spontaneous, interruptive birdsongs;
playful cold that awakens; a memory regained:
we lie on our bed of memory,
under winter grey,
accepting gold caught in the web
woven through the turn of the seasons;
my broken dove,
lie softly on your mended wing,
brought now into awareness,
for in its fissure lies representative my heart
newly awake, to,
with the seasoning of grief,
be brought again,
close to knowing and holding.

Camellia Words

In the heavy hours following midday,
I dream, antidotedly,
but I do not dream that you will come again,
for you have journeyed to a circumstance
that does not allow return.
And in the disposition I have left you,
until a softer hour.
And so in this hesitating, late afternoon,
I looked to find, and gathered,
a sunset-hued camellia,
from its tree we planted in a spring
when it was small
and we were strong.
Its petals looked up to me,
moving with my touch,
becoming your lips speaking to me;
a wind passed by
and the petals continued to tremble,
with the press of flame red.
The light became shadowed
and I could not see when the petals did not speak.
You have loosed the gates,
unraveled and smoothed the knot,
and you have come to me: a flower today,
the sunlight on the dew in coming hours,
the wind bringing the warm gardenia,
the rain to quiet and refresh,
to encourage the newness in tomorrow.
In Martha's dress, I tended food and drink,

and did not sit long enough, with ease,
at your feast,
to hear, in strong and weighted tones,
what now the petals whisper;
my heart hears, but with difficulty,
for mortal words lift delicately from petaled lips.
But so, true, in gentle light.

The Anticipatory Sting

It is hard to look into the eye
that itself sees death;
there is a resignation,
an emptiness that closings leave.
The clasp is genuine,
though without strength,
as spoken words that fall away,
coarse, unhappy sounds.
Excrement is tinted with antiseptic and powders,
placed and hidden away,
and it is difficult to know
if the flowers are to cheer or to mourn.
Perhaps the darkest moment,
even more than the moment of release,
is the turning away,
in the path of his tenuous breath,
to walk out of his wasting world to life,
our life,
that commodity that in buying and selling,
we yet have acceptable gold,
and his is lost-
old, unhealthy,
without salvation,
irredeemably lost.

The Ineffective Patte

The closing day brings a quietness,
and in this hour a shadowed remembrance of your
quiet
when your world began to be dark.
And so, my thoughts run,
over one and then the other,
wishing to find, perhaps the pauline beauty in pathos;
I found, then, the Christmas of that year of your quiet.
My heart whispered to me
that the beautiful festival this year
would not shine or sound again;
and with measured effort,
I went into the attic;
and I stood the tree,
and it did stand.
I placed the decorations with a grieving care,
my heart bowed low
as I recalled the circumstance of each ornament.
And when the tree stood, handsome and lighted,
the nurse and I brought you in and asked your
pleasure;
you looked full into the tree,
and to either side,
and we knew you did not, at all, see.
Like a sad melody, dark and soft,
our tears fell into your quietness and dark.
If I could have made a patte,
to anoint your eyes,
indeed, your ravaged body,

but you needed a savior,
with as much love
but, yet, a waiting grace.
The path out of life is a given
wrenching from ourselves, a crucifixion,
yet that of hell which is death,
but I cannot receive the wisdom in yours.

Faery Gold

Tonight I lift my brush,
and it bleeds out you;
and so I take up my pen
only for the words to settle in blood of you;
I come then to select works and words,
to ponder their truths,
and my eyes bleed forth those truths of you.
I am mortal yet,
but my thoughts do not forget other worlds.
I can know of crusades,
and chapels, and the fig tree;
and over them composes a golden mist
with borders of deep violent and crimson.
I feed on the food of angels
remembering when I once shared
a rose breath,
in the springtime,
with one who unveiled beauty,
a complete beauty,
that can lie between recognition and loss.
And there is, over this beautiful memory,
so that it is completely covered,
a golden veil,
protecting and keeping,

with borders of deep violet and crimson;
within move two figures,
one as handsome and strong
as a fine brass instrument,
the other as the lovely blue gross of Venice,
catching light, moving the blueness
as the continuous pulsating of a heart-
a heart that has loved.

That my love for you at the first
has not found complete expression
leaves me with a fullness
that moves intention to spill out,
and so words come, to begin,
that speak of our thousand days.
Reflected in your eyes
was a kind of awe
and a gentleness in giving and taking,
and it was good to please.
Beside you I came to again have definition,
and I stood tall enough to meet your smile.
There was a splendid excitement when we touched,
and the anticipation of hours together
was reborn with each adventure.
You loved me before I let down my hair,
and in that faith
I shook it all out,
perfumed with water and fragrant soaps.
Wine and music were sweet,
prompting weeping at the understanding of darkness;
speaking often of truth,
we dealt in loyalties and symbol.
I love you still,
but my love is now more like the candle's light
at the close of a beautiful day;
it stands as would a bright soldier,
touched by shadows and dark.
I must carry this ember into my night,
lest the shadow and dark blind and maim me,
making me smaller,

for the present is more because of what is past:
I have asked the dove and the strawberry
to speak for us,
to enlarge the light,
for they are beautiful
and hold quiet passion.
Fragrant powders of rose and olive will be selected
and their softness
sprinkled over the leaves
of the berry and the dove's wings
to establish our carnality,
our realness
to these framing true days of our Camelot.

The Love Bearing

First grief passes in his own personal season,
with dark mourning weeds laid aside,
but its face remains,
a visage out of more comfortable garments,
to fellowship with days of anniversary,
when new, welcomed tears are gathered:
in the time of bramble green,
of the day the prodigal returns;
when locust and potato vines are warm,
in hours knowing the glory of the japonica,
its reflecting the distant sunset,
that it can be held,
marvelously,
its petals lying upon each other,
together,
opening, as do lips,
forming words, sayings,
close and passionate;
beauty leans on the arm of loss,
walking timorously between holding and failing,
but finding, in this fashioning,
the circumstance for other,
attending beauty,
for beauty is beauty given,
stirrings felt and understood,
gifts out of shadow and dark.
And so,
in a season offering
pain remembered is found

a treasure of newness,
a rebirth of feature and gesture,
for tears pour out closeness,
that but lately brought into being,
tears rich,
a wealth to be caught and measured,
as silver and diamonds,
their heaviness becoming a gift,
our bending a bearing of love.

The Arranging

A late afternoon's arranging early spring blossoms,
camellia and azalea,
companioning in late afternoon,
their pattern faltering,
falling softly aside,
my hands patiently lifting and placing,
enjoying, feeding,
bringing again hours spent in hungry embraces,
moments calling forth soft apology,
and comfortable intimacies;
in the journeyed road of passion,
reaching toward holding,
need growing into giving,
sensation and thought becoming the flower
an earlier, quickening glimpse
had painted flame and closing sunset;
and with the falling,
arranging blossoms,
the beauty calling up these such spoken images,
came the ambassador of sorrow,
a tear full of loss,
a veil of silk that covers the beauty,
embellishing,
to hold it into another opening
of waiting, compassionate hours.

Early spring, Richard,
so much, so many –

March Reverie

A solemn quietness fills my rooms;
the clock is gentle but deliberate.
The daisies and carnations, with their grace and color,
silently struggle with my wistful, growing melancholy.
The music is without sound;
the lights seem pale, lacking in their familiar
brilliance.
And the air forms a heavy square around me.
I know, again, that you are not here,
and that I walk a measured, patterned walk.
I fancy that if only I would throw open the doors,
you would be there, the center to all the darkness in
the grande heavens.
But you would have in your hands the sun and the
moon and stars.
You would fling them against the darkness for me,
and I would smile, now in my abundant light.
My hands would be desperate to touch you;
close to my face, you would smile your chestnut smile,
and I would weep.
And then, like a soft glow that has faded, you would be
gone away again,
and I would court my grief.
We so wish for the corporeal, for we want to hold what
is ours.
But the soul, in its truest for, is alone of flesh.
We can touch it only as we touch the sunlight and the
silver in the moon.

And our darkness can then be hushed and made
somewhat softer.
Unhappily, we must strive mightily with ourselves,
with will and truth,
so that we may touch the gold in sunlight
and perhaps smile into the fragile nature of a
moonbeam.

Adagio Hope

In these adagio hours, those slowly quiet and dark,
when I wrestle with sleep, the key laid apart,
I rise to let the darkness accompany my journey into
sorrow;
for I will hear again chapel voices and sanctuary
organ music that remind me,
pull out of me my knowing soul, and finally to devour
its temple;
only then can I return to my bed, spent in the beautiful
pain of memory,
exhausted and empty, to sleep and build the sacrifice
again.
For grief is more than the day, and more than the
night;
it fills up the veins and pulsates the heart;
it dampens the eye and shadows the smile;
it is born of loss, and spilled blood is always empty;
more, a loss is never again truly filled, only rearranged,
with hope,
so that the chapel bells will be heard in the hunt, and
not in the cell.

The Afterward

Water music and sunlight
ignite a busy, quiet spectacle of recollected days,
promises and expectations
toward the right and the good.
Fragrances bring again warm smiles,
the turning kaleidoscope of truth,
a suggested pleasing to be known in my berry colors:
a malady's different turn,
or perhaps a late mourning–
My chronicle
is that filled up with grandly humble movements,
but they touch my awareness now
as memorable hours spent in royalty and reverence.
The bloom is full so soon,
and the tender, blest rain of spring loses its fervor
with the greening of the countryside.
Indeed, rain into dust and the grey cold
is our receiving of a flat silence,
and in a great sense, the afterward.

My Company

Aria and moonglow awaken
to a haunting melody
that carries over ribbons of lighted darkness,
through valleys of warm velvet,
rising to hills just below words that fell about,
rich tenor sounds,
words that brought me again to you.
It was easy to hear the words,
to bend with the familiar pain of your
absence;
the darkness held me in gentle,
supporting arms;
the words prepared my heart,
and I visited you,
moonlight and quiet
becoming the balm to my sweet wound.
And so,
balsam and red are once more my company,
and I have touched you;
pain has allowed relationship,
in place,
gathered by the ear,
the shell collecting,
watering again sea-soil,
soul-soil,
the waiting,
hungry sentiments of my heart.

Among Autumn's First:
Stones One (Morning)

I thought to have lost you, further, still, to another day,
no calling
images, no silent words reminding; but evening
shadows can
offer up secrets, and a voice at a distance which I could
not place
or measure, told me of stepping stones, rounds of
pebble finish,
their circumference pattering in my eye. And I went to
their grave,
their casting off, to time, now two decades and more,
their tender
care of the seasons, covered over by straw, leaves, and
the earth,
it clinging to, giving bosom to their neglect, and they
were felt, and
were alive again.

I lifted away their cloak of natural threads, cloth in
umbers and grey,
and with gentle purpose, troubled the soil that held
their place,
as the voice whispered to my memory;
"Oh Richard, they look up to me, mirroring your strong
hands placing them; oh Richard, come again in these
spaces where
parameters are soft, in neutral colors, where love's
effort is not so

great, for time, and its very able lieutenants of activity, growing
thought, and the wisdom of all those who will not bear the very loss
of thee, a wager difficult to the keeping of thee."
Blest eventide, shadows and the bell ringing of love distanced to the Shenandoah.
The sunrise, the setting sun: oh Richard, do not forget to call, to
whisper, to ring, for more and more, I must, with my heart's saying,
out of the reservoir of ours, the industry of keeping burdened to
thee, the ringing of bells, the many voices of those whose procession
this time, are, yet, spirit and soul, for in my place, that of memory is
cast, if with some reticence, to the certain away.

Elizabeth, 9/22/2001
Image carried since late yesterday, the first day of Autumn, September 21 –

Among Autumn's First:
Stones Two (Afternoon)

*In the years of then, what sweet games we played, in
moments
that knew most fragile, lifting butterflies, that with
difficulty of
wills' confusion, dissolution, and deep yearning for the
first
gardenias' morning warmth, their truly passing,
bringing an
almost futility, and more, with resolve out of
dependences
we did not understand, of angels lighted or demons
clever of
darkness – we found echoes, and held to them, and
gathered
small treasures in their continuous, circling light –*

*These secrets I find now, your conversation silent, but
the voice of
the hawk's cry, distancing in the upward expanse of
reaching
Bamboo, its lost planting found again in its more,
pebbled stones
of your placement, realized of earthen smooth and in
umbered
grey flora, clothing from these years, of your closed
voice; under
your grapevine, even, there, it of your last pleasure, in
the now*

of Autumn, in the time since, and the "Pathetique"
knows, of your
finding, knows close, in the now of falling from
noonday to me.

After unearthing stepping stones around the patio,
placed by
Richard, his own wanting, forgotten until they imaged
several
days ago: oh September, you have given me, and I am
in
constant mourning, as your dying echo of summer
radiance;
I have always been so, and so, why.

Elizabeth, 9/22/2001

Among Autumn's First:
Stones Three (Early Evening)

*In a familiar returning, I arrived into the Westward
and the setting sun;
and with some careful dissonance, I knew it not to be
in spacing,
familiar, hued more an apology of polite yellow than a
fire of gold,
more a continuing moment of glaring than a largo in a
spreading fan.*

*In a sudden recognition, of curious juxtaposition, the
often accepted
true of feminine tedium quite had failed the advent of
Autumn, the
departing summer, in moments full the day, having
given its
radiance to weep into accepted glow.*

*And I brought the goodbye to your stones, their
morning unearthing
left to eventide, and their bringing into today of their
sleep of
yesterday: water rushing, pulsating, purposeful again,
in small
azalea, whose twines and roots held from larger hosts
above,
re-discovered, yet new, in their below, to the stones, a
juxtaposition spoken into the bringing pebble faces,
the casting*

away the blossom, the care of birthing neglect, years unobserved,
of exquisite layering, the rich earth born in seasons of sun and rain.

Oh Richard, oh Richard, in your comings to me, in the now, seldom,
and rare, with their pressing knowing, my heart must, with care,
receive, for the growing seasons tender as they distance, and I
cannot certain that in the nightfall I will carry the peace I have
gathered until this time of your stones, placed with your hands,
mine alone now, collected as September jewels for my arranging,
alone, with my hands in tomorrow's September sunlight.

Elizabeth, 9/22/2001

The Strawberry Kiss

I was about, making a coffee,
when I became aware of the strawberry,
your thoughtful little gift to me,
from a visit out of town.
It sits happily on the stove cabinet,
bright red
with little black seeds pushing up all over.
It pleased me then, and it does even now,
that you brought it gently to me.
There were so many years that we did not
understand how to please each other:
all of the unhappy Christmas presents;
the lovely golden rod I gathered
and innocently brought inside;
and the many heroic and suggestive toilet waters
I selected for you that lacked somehow
or were not altogether acceptable.
You fared with more harmony than I,
for you came to learn
that little bits and favors of nature
touched and pleasured me;
and in the last days we had together,
you were generous indeed
with these gifts and expressions.
The bitter kiss of the strawberry
is that the effort, the resolve,

the gift was so late,
as the playing out of a beautiful,
but somehow unfortunately visited denouement:
the feelings, then, that I hold today are mixed,
so that, in conclusion,
I am left with a shadow of sadness.

Written not long after Richard's death (2-3 years)
The strawberry I have still,
the sentiment still, but
not now so much sadness with it
11-16-2002

The Wren and the Peacock

My cry was soft,
but I wished to see myself,
the pattern I was,
how I stood in the presence of the sun.
And so the sketch began.
My musings presented a center, a heart,
but in building the image,
your strength was used.
The composition struggled with the unhappy condition
lying between my day's wishes
sitting on your porches.
Ah, Olive, I live yet
and you were left thin, transparent and dying.
The wren had allowed his strength
in the accomplishment of the peacock.
What sorrow in the fear,
the sleeping eyes of the wren.

Thee Is

*Thee is the gentle ache in my heart's
closeted part;
Thee is a familiar shadow that
knows my steps,
and, to soften these midnights.
Thee is the omelet of morning
sunlight,
and dew of flowers;
Thee is the smile I find when I
gather summer fruit,
full roundness and remembered
colors,
to taste and know their warm
radiance.
Such whispers of Thee are, once and
again, laid aside, covered over,
by mummerings,
but Thee is not far from
me,
For Thee is forever returning,
in the characters of
jeweled days and
hallowed nights.*

Elizabeth
early/later

I heard a German chorus today,
voices that expressed the great allelujah at death,
just as I felt sounded
at the moment your spirit left its worn dwelling,
to venture into the world beyond.
You must forgive,
but there occurs, especially at these such times,
a need for mourning,
including that I know of you,
that you in some fashion, be with me.
And so, I imagine
that you move and enjoy sentiments.

I see you positioned atop a grande pyramid,
your bow taunt,
eager to dislodge its arrow.
I fancy that you move with the wind,
and find comfortable a nearness to the sun;
that satyrs and unicorns sit down with you,
to enjoy fruit from the rainbow's colors.
The moon has become your lady,
and you lie welcomed in her soft illumination,
her shadows gradually to be pulled over,
securing your contentment.
I imagine that there exist
no clowns in your company;
there is no need to exaggerate features
and other grotesque realities
to cover the even more fearful true self.
Laughter has a harsh quality,
a foolish quality,

and so the softness from the twinkling stars
causes you to smile, happily, without explanation.

I do not let the thought be announced
that all may not be as I surmise.
In our days together,
it was as though you were, innocently,
the offering for some great wrong,
plodding into darkness
that offered only a tortuous emptiness.
My wish is that with the marvelous allelujah
that unbearable condition was mediated.
It is pitiable that I can do little else
than to wish for you what I know,
and those things I consider beneficial and good.
Perhaps, somehow, I will come to know
that your peace and pleasure
are of those things other than I can imagine.
Though couched in earthly descriptions,
these your movements and sentiments
do, indeed, carry you further away from me.
But then, whether in earthly nothingness
or celestial fullness,
I have only, have, always, had only
what could be fancied
from the distant self you showed me.
It will be then, when you are above me,

and the rainfall is gentle,
and when the moon, at last, awakens,
just before I sleep,
that I will know your smile
and I will remember, again, yet, still.
And it will not matter,
the impotent, unending silence.

May Fullness

Come to me in the May month, and I
be a flower in your hands.
My heart will be as warm as
a new sun,
and my petaled lips will open crimson
to you;
The sighs from my passion will touch
your eyes and carry the sweetness
of the honeysuckle.
My devotion will smile to you
until sunset
when my petals fall to my
kindly chaperone – ever biding,
silently,
requiring patient justice,
the wager of glory and ashes.
I speak
with passion gentle:
I will be for you a season of fullness
when you come to me in the
May month.

Elizabeth
Early 1990's

Reflections

Lost Rapture

I feel, in these closing hours of the day, very weary,
as if I am dragging along an oppressive fatigue.
I feel that I have been poured out of myself so that I am
a great nothing.
And not for any exalted reason, with which I might be
comforted.
Indeed, I am almost without care of reason, to find it,
see it, or be comforted by it.
My thoughts have been unhappy, of the little foxes that
show how we come
to know that our colors, in good light, are old and no
longer thrive.
We spend time quietly laying aside dreams that
require strengths we hope for,
but even with pitiable searching, cannot now find.
The heroic names we were given at birth now seem,
somehow, inappropriate,
for we are not now heroic;
the bursting rose within, in our chest, that expectancy,
the almost mystical beauty of which we feel all the
world rose each morning
to glimpse and from which to be enriched, is near
death, in rapture,
so that it has given over to the thorn, living but tasting
of bitter.

It is good that days conclude; perhaps tomorrow it will
not matter
that the rose is given shadow by the thorn, for lest we
lose our way,
we must hold that we have known,
the rapture, the touch and smile of the rose.

Fancy Noir

A portion of yesterday comes to mind,
a darkened fancy that I danced with a cat.
It was warm and black,
and sleek and soft;
and I felt its heart catch the rhythm of my own.
But the familiar refuge of reason did not sustain me,
and I know, in reflection,
that I have colored you black
and into a cat form.
For truly, with you,
I can dance only at a distance,
and any warmness and closeness
are the precious yield of careful words.
Once again, you are cut away;
your heart cannot ever again catch the rhythm of
mine.
Unhappy dancing cat,
alive and real in fancy alone,
a messenger from the heart of him,
who in fancy, you were.

Music fills my rooms,
touching and shadowing,
first beauty with a haunting past,
flowing melancholy
that holds the lovely pain of dying rose,
a rose whose face finds a fading hue of loss,
establishing beauty both noble and lasting,
to be scripted into melodies
that remind and awaken,
into dyes and mediums
that will hold her eternal.
In conversation,
leaves fall,
and with an unknowing,
a freedom that allows their splendid finale,
quite impervious
to our unsubtle, and paltry domination
of time's constancy and record.
In my hand I hold again my heart,
a very nearness to the other side of closing,
and still,
still I wish to remain among my toys,
and arrange, for beauty, in its very passion,
waits to yet arouse and seduce,
that she fill me up as would an able lover,
and in that embrace,
we to wander far into pleasure,
and when spent beyond another
such accepting and quickening struggle,
then will I allow thee,
my heart,

to lie lifeless in my hand.

How to say, how to say -- the heart
full into heavy burdening;
feel, know, remember –
catch, lose, lost –
please no, to forget,
yes, to forget: the gardenia, reminding left-
over passion in early
morning walks,
while others slept,
but the gardenia, in petaled gowns
of sweetest velvet snow.
How to say,
a burden heavy so,
gardenia in this moment now, of those moments then,
dry, of summer warmth, of mornings' mist,
fragrance, innocence's death,
in tenses passing still,
in collections, passed.

Elizabeth
May 19, 2003
On hearing "Time To Say Goodbye"
On May 18, 2003,
In thoughts, quiet, until their release with the
poignant sentiment, remembering,
mine and Richard's thirty-third
anniversary, May 30, 1970 –

1967, April 14, on Mitchell Avenue

Companion Dove

I know today that I fly alone,
without my companion dove.
We are deeply into autumn
and rain has brought a close melancholy.
Soon light will bid important travelers
to journey the distance home,
to sit by the fire,
a fire of their particular own.
I will need only an humble fire,
and the cup will not be necessary,
since its dark bouquet
compliments best a companion.
For the evening's amusement I will ponder,
with excitement,
that one of my clowns is turned askew,
and not as I remember placing it.
How warming and delicious
that someone might be or has been in my rooms.
And then, as the evening embraces all of the night,
I concede that I placed the clown askew,
only not to remember.
I will, then, further my acquaintance with the night;
there is now a camaraderie between us,
becoming so through many hours of quiet reflection;
my thoughts dance in the darkness
and are held up for acceptance or rejection,
mercifully to be accepted or rejected,
thrown into a bag of stars and dust
where they may appear brighter at another time.

Indeed, I often feel
that my soul is a flowing darkness,
a forever night.
And truly, yes, I know
that I fly in the darkness alone,
without my companion dove.

Midnight Whisper

At the pre-eminent,
the transcendent twelfth hour,
at midnight,
I did not hear the dead moan,
or catch glimpses of souls
moving through the spheres;
I only dined on waffles with strawberry topping,
and coffee warmed over from the morning,
now eighteen hours past.
Just as I sat at table,
the sounds of a beautiful, melancholy
in theme
came very close to me.
In this beautiful setting,
I struggled to find some ease with myself,
as I am,
against some background.
There is, however, no background,
for I am free of institution and schedule;
and so, there is not any one to recount the day to,
and flowers placed in our bedroom
appear apathetic for lack of admiring glances.
Hours without you pass by me
as if from another world,
a world forgetful of you.
Friends and acquaintances
have moved you away into memory,
and we speak of you as an historical figure.

It may be that the past does hold you,
but at selected times
you are loaned to my present, at usury, and dear.
For I see myself tonight,
with midnight waffle,
and in my freedom,
yet wishing for your chestnut presence,
your full smile,
against the background of all we were;
it is only that the hour and setting,
and we players,
are not anymore in place.
The night has a splendor,
a portion of which is a lovely, haunting sadness.
It is the dark carpet
on which I draw my postures
that will bring you to me;
and so, I softly protest.
I cannot go gentle into this night,
without some promise of a caring, moonlit whisper.

You did sleep,
and then, with a quick punctuation of it
you did sleep unto finality.
I held your hand,
and you let go,
the last clasp.
It was done quickly,
and I knew suddenly a darkness,
a stretching out of time with anticipation
smoothed away into a nothingness.
You had been quiet in it all,
but the silent conversations, our last embraces,
now cry out
at their leave-taking and in their absence.
I cannot see you now,
but I know,
and that knowledge is like a brilliant portion
of hanging tapestry that shows us together,
the punctuation and all that was in it,
rescinded,
and our hands hold again each other.

A comforting penning of my loss of the good with Richard –
at Christmastime, I think, several years ago.

No Bride Will

Ebbing and flowing, altogether one season,
only just roses of light and dark,
of love and the casting off fixed necessity:
hearing my dearest souls out days long, silently long
in their absolute brevity, bringing
in sudden, old darkness,
you come, in suspended whisper,
to know in me again that which you once drew,
as the whimsical joy of the spider's
weaving, to, for your own,
beauty in innocence,
in loyalty, in lessons of wonder and devotion
to the tender and fierce natural:
in will which insisted, and brought dreams
into our struggling hands.
And thou who found me in that helpless
spring, mine, that season, holding a
haunting soul malaise, of which thou, whose
softest resonance touches now on my cheek,
come to be its healing potion;
and thou whose dreams had must to die,
that honor be found again, against demons which
lie dead upon thy ashes, their sacrificial
nourishment left wanting.

In sounds which bear neither wind nor light,
or berries hanging in fanciful gleaming,
nor petals whose softness finds
arranging's glory,

these do, yet, gather as shadow, in voice and
instrument;
and the pain of words in a catastrophic
colliding –
this pain of absence, this pain of presence –
let the nightingale forget to mourn the twilight,
the rose, to sing a new lament of my heart,
newly again,
fully torn,
breathing Autumn's warm sweet olive,
a gold washing of all I am left with.

And no bride will wear a dress of white satin,
with hanging white silk,
but with sewn lace of ecrued roses,
about even others,
ecrued,
their hosting drape, bouqueted lilies of
the valley,
old flesh in new ribbon,
fainting in its flowing –
for there is not world, save mine,
cast in these rooms of fading gold,
to ebb and flow
into gardenia
the hue of memory in the far away,

allthewhile drifting, yet, still away,
almost into winter's umbered grey.

Elizabeth, November 11, 2001, at
about 12:30 am –
Images that came just before, and when hearing
Foster and Allen,
with deepest weeping:
Mamma, Daddy, and Richard –

"Do You Think You Could Love Me Again"

Continuing Anguish

I have sat, alone, to listen and hear
the indescribable beauty
of the violin in its concerto.
It calls out of me heavy weeping,
deep crimson tears
to fall onto my garments,
which if seen,
would fashion a crimson tribute to my lost loves.
But the eyes in my rooms have no soul,
and so there is none to comfort me,
no reverence save mine.
It is of others, however,
that my tears fall:
those and our hours of coming together,
tender moments with good laughter,
and then knowing and saying good-bye.
I would take my garments
and fold together the fallen tears saved,
the violin's words,
and offer the gift to the heavens
that my own not despair of my remembrance.
Oh night! Sadly marked,
wandering dove,
you pour out of your darkness to my grief,
so that I am most an instrument of mourning,
and with loss and its nothingness
my concert sounds forth
in empty, continuing anguish.

During the memorial eve,
I lighted a candle;
I looked into its flame,
and it reached up to me.
Within the white wax I saw a crimson flower,
such as your heart,
and the flame touched me
so that I felt a moment of true pain.
The flame will die,
and your heart will return
to moments that I do not know.
But I know first grief that the flame bore
the strength of a funeral pyre,
that I could receive its touch enough
to know your presence in the flower.
How grateful, my soul,
that gracious angels will, indeed, snuff the flame
and close the eyes of the flower,
for the eve is but one darkness,
with all to follow
generous hours of healing, usurping
a Thisbe complexion.

A hawk's cry in the gathering August warmth;
the morning grows into its fullness,
and the truth of the day presses forth:
you are not here,
and cannot be.
You rise with the cry
and I know your distance.
Years pass,
with the gold,
the heat,
the cry,
and you are not here.
But in the intimacy of the cry,
there is possible,
perhaps,
a wholeness,
for the strength of struggle in passion
knows a pause,
a quiet, bittersweet reprieve of time and distance,
with assurance that the hawk flies
in a space that echoes life
and the governance of accepting memory.

Pastoral Songs

The essence of a choice beauty
rarely offers more than the gold
found is remembered days of pastorals sweet,
which in themselves,
wore beauty in its first fullness,
with the joyous innocence of beginnings.
Holding these is as daylight's urgency
in the unconditional presence of coming dark,
having fallen from noon,
lingering entergy,
royalty cast aside,
to dance with frantic care,
within hurried hours of grace,
and know the shadow,
finding jewels that lie, together there,
falling onto surfaces
that arrange and appear as dark,
to be an Appomattox wedding
with the schedule of hours:
the sword of day to the hand of night,
weeping dew
forever chronicling the ceremony.
The images of memory
do not sing with great voice,
but that of their voice is utterance worthy,
beyond almost any merit
assigned or sanctioned,
for their songs review and mend,
and place the dead,

altogether providing salvation
for living thought
inside failing flesh,
the decay serving fragrance
about remembered pastorals
and their luted songs
that wander into falling light.

Sweet Shadow

The hour of moments that do not sigh,
that know beauty and satisfied yearnings,
these fail to hear a coming silence,
dark finding light,
shadows covering without.
But what glory within the shadow,
for it frames the beauty,
the satisfied yearnings,
to, finally, with the rarest caress,
rest gently on their face,
to, by its covering,
draw their soul with their absence.
Sweet, then, is the bringing of shadows,
that we not forget the nature of our good,
which is to begin its flight in its fullest presence,
the monarch into its building gold;
sweet shadow,
that we not need to pierce our eyes,
to hide,
in our blindness,
their knowing loss,
but only to cast about
onto the gentle smile
inside the healing compassion of grey,
granting fading radiance given over to its second

newness,
found through is storing,
long with patience
in the road of memory.

Reference to beautiful Irish piece.
-the gift of time to consider and gather,
to prepare and accept loss

Oh Then

I have passed through
and today my roses bloom,
their fragrance firing again
my still innocent heart, now barren,
bringing a spring, beautifully constant,
of bittersweet thought.
But then... oh then...
– a time washed of fresh cranberry,
shadowed about by forgotten gold,
banished now to the distant provinces
and gardens of yesterday and memory –
Yet it was... it was...
It came to be and it was.
And then... oh then...
Like sunlight, your tears awakened me,
and in your joy starred my own,
my sunlight, my own.

Richard was a complex, tortured individual;
in the first, good years,
I learned to be unhappy when he was,
and in the rare moments of his happiness,
I was so happy too.

This Larceny

The day has spoken to me,
letting me know
that I have lost you to reason,
for time has provided memory
a net of poignant scenes,
to stand watchman
over those sentiments of you.
And so, a great darkness did settle down,
but the sun is a formidable warrior,
and a smile now covers over,
dispelling the drifting grey,
while allowing shadows beyond the trees,
with the starlight,
so that my heart does not in this larceny
weep first tears.

My heart weeps again, as if the first,
its tears falling, yearning for
a catching with where they
may rest as all together, a staid
monument to my ever grief.
Could, more, smoke and dead fire of ashes
cover me, I would fell in appropriate
attire,
and my words would issue forth
an accompanying dirge.
These postures become erect, inside the chambers of my
heart,
when circumstance is oblivious to its
many stings. Residual hurt in
unattractive guises, alongside present
pain and failing hope, look to the
will of tears as my heart's immortality.

Elizabeth
January 1, 2007

Difficult day and dark thoughts;
I fear the night for it has become,
over and again, a journey of anguish,
finally into light, fatigued, pressed, but must.
The day had been joyful,
beginning of the other side of memory,
and I, with a dark invitation,
move under a sombre covering.
As the hours came to enjoy their freedom,
I apportioned shares of the sun to myself,
and the covering softened
with each slice of brightness,
only to settle darkly
as the night fills up my windows.
With more strength than the scream
that has lost its fear,
the appetite that ravages reason and gold,
and the fire unbasketed,
eating green and wooden scapes, hungrily,
mood is to be acknowledged.
It supports the will to rise,
the courage to do battle,
the fire to love,
and it can weaken underneath
even the forordained.
And if the mood be fair,
golden, yet angelic,
we smile,
seeing what we wish in all things;
but should it be grey,
the laughter's complexion hollow,

we may, as many, turn to impatient suggestion,
perhaps potions and prayers,
that the melody be touched and kissed,
praise to praise,
quite forgetting of the shadowed largo.

I stood shaken,
in another realization
of how final is his leave-taking;
on other days,
in other rooms,
I have known,
but in each is a new closing.
Perhaps it will eat itself away,
tearing over and again
and the leave-taking
will be left a lighted darkness,
a void without a greyed center.
Shadows will lean into it,
and only then will the pain touch me.

He was my warrior,
and because his wars were of such magnitude,
such fierceness,
in accepting the glove
he stood magnificent,
altogether glorious,
requiring devotion perpetual.

Reminding Rose

I carried a rose throughout the night,
its complexion and petal silks
becoming pale, and deep,
differently arranging,
but holding to its self
so that I knew it and loved it;
but I did not rouse and write,
and with the cleansing of morning light,
it has joined the great congregation
of image and thought
that sleeps behind full knowing.
Often and again,
we do not rouse and write,
and the beauty of selected hours,
increasing into its gathering,
is allowed to fulfill
beyond our collected, familiar rapture.
Like the snow above Garmish,
with the constant,
and comfortable distancing train,
with good bread and cheese,
and warm spring wine,
its beauty at departure,
in its complete realization,
was ours,
to become within the hour,
lost,
slipped away,

into an impression
touched by a small sorrow:
that it, with patience,
and a modest indignation,
reminds.

New Desert

Deep, breathless words,
rich tones and round sounds,
the night's color,
raven all without,
and the poetry of yesteryear sings;
they were as the words,
years too beautiful to stay,
their sweetness,
the center,
the throat
out of which passed their spirit,
leaving silence.
The color of crimson,
following the movement of my fingers,
resting inside gold,
finds anniversary,
memory of wine and laughter,
special effort holding a small spring
inside gathering neutral colors,
uneasy scarlet,
pouring sands
of coming desert hours and quieted fire.
Again words,
carrying desperate passion,
a treasure of gold,
a memorial to yesterday's desert
that came to fill empty hours,
but the desert yet in some part full,
bearing a longing

whose cries fell tears
that found a voice of beautiful dark;
- new desert filling these hours,
now, with new emptiness,
new silence entering dark;
my crimson,
inside gold,
knows my hand, only,
and is deaf
to today's laughter, beside wine.

Ninth Anniversary

1992-2001
December 15-16, 1992

The day must weep its parting, for the dark rose
of midnight breathes near to fullness;
and the day after anniversary
has forgotten, the greater part, silent tears
which found it, in the night,
in early winter, knowing present, already,
festival and holiday.
Nightsounds, in spirited, jocund chase, sing faint
echoes of their voice, in their truest season,
and winds, more than soft constancy,
remind chimes, those, which in certainty,
explain mountain temple bells,
but together with clay from unschooled hands,
discover unfortunate catcher-pieces
sounding a willing, but silvered control to.
Peace begs a room, a chamber inside the undrawn,
the altogether tangled, and with wisdom
confused, knot of my heart,
and while this circumstance is the portion
for which I beg, in great anguish,
I cannot, until I must, when there is no longer
any choice, bloom and fire, light and knowing,
but only closing, into these their
closing, into their dying, anniversary –
oh shadow of mourning,

in the fading out of browntoned and grey –
washed anniversary,
--into this room, this only chamber, can I
impotently open to my begging.

12-16-2001
Jonah came today,
my poor Jonah –

Uneven Healing

Passing the night
and awaiting the first light of day,
has been rather like
patiently opening a well wrapped gift.
I came downstairs just after midnight
and reflected on how happily the day had been spent.
The hours visiting in Summit
had been a warm experience.
I realized that what I was reviewing
was the culmination of healing.
For several years,
and most intensely in recent months,
the long hours of recuperation
had included despair, struggle, resolve and hope,
all rising and falling on each other.
My physical healing
has been less than what was wished for,
but it has provided time and circumstance
for the healing of my soul.
Long stored bitterness
has eroded portions of my warm spirit
that were once pleasant and good.
We cannot hold all to our ledger, our scales,
for we, ourselves, are already wanting.
In coming to know thus,
we can be made more really whole,
even without a reminiscent scar.

And we took the train to Venice,
out of Munich,
at the exact midnight hour;
and I had not known death, other than it housed in
metaphor,
either gracious or unkind,
until your love's first hesitation, to grow into refusal,
and final spurning.
Could these have been spoken or penned of a villain
to one pure,
the verse would have stood well,
but they were words of you,
and you were not ever, to my heart,
Villain, but him into whose our adagio I gave
my only breath;
I could not find it back again for your first
and holding, tender touch,
that of gardenia in triangular warmth,
your key of movement radiance opened
my coming, willing soul,
out into a filling bondage without any
leaving, helping soulwinds.

--Daffodils, yellowbells, snowdrops, tears
in their distance, or perhaps
in fatigue of effort to hold,
in warmth or chill,
requiring the beautiful wounding brought of music
and fragrance, their abundant dalliance into

yesterday, calling
forth full dew,
and its fraternity with knowing,
full, again,
in these moments now,
full bittersweet.

Begun 2/1/2002 with recording a memory, perhaps its first, of our
overnight train from Munich to Venice
in the 1980's;
Other thoughts came of our early days
together, their assessment,
coupled with spring notes taken in
this week –
finding loss in beauty past, wishing
to know it again;
even in the pain, aware of its
absence,
wishing still.

Elizabeth, 2/2/2002

Not In My Hand

I know it and it touches me,
but it is outside of me,
being looked in upon,
always a frame of the flowing past,
within the shadowed glass of death,
greyed by the winds of silence:
a still,
with an ableness yet to touch.
That not in my hand,
I cannot let go,
and not again,
in its flower,
its passion,
in its first roundness and wholeness,
can it,
even with desperate purpose and struggle,
be held.

Grief of Richard,
just two-three years ago:
anniversary time-
Elizabeth, 2000-2001

Catching a moment,
thoughts are held,
and the clock pours out
a generous, true knowing:
in dry straw falling,
in leaves finding the wind,
and lifting into final, brown journeys;
in the constant light,
leaning into its fullness.
Like a beloved sister,
quiet enters,
a white shadow,
as a silk berceuse,
to hold,
just inside the light.
And the violin's sentiment.
With the finding of sweet melodies,
the past wanders into the ripe frame,
and we know,
with the truth of Quasimodo's rose,
the wealth in loss,
and the plenty in the golden dance of now.

Lost "Pathetique"

The music had been especially lovely, since the soft,
twilight hours.
And then I thought to hear the "Pathetique", your
"Pathetique".
I was so captured by the idea of your "Pathetique"
and my memory of the many hours we had spent
listening and enjoying this composition,
I was not aware early that the piece I was hearing
might not, perhaps, be the Tchaikovsky piece.
But then I became aware of my uncertainty,
and I was suddenly grieved in knowing how much has
been forgotten.
Oh, my dear! Is this the way, of health, contentment,
that I become confused, in distant reflection,
so that I do not anymore truly know Your
"Pathetique"?
With inventory, I learned that the piece just heard
was, indeed, the "Pathetique", your "Pathetique",
but that I should be at all uncertain, therein lies my
grief.

In these moments
Love is close to me;
it is a knowing,
an understanding.
Joy hangs about all my rooms,
as if, almost to slip away.
I know, closely, the nature of my walk,
that it will reach into the longest darkness
when I will know only the moment,
and yesterday will have become
a long quiet and shadowed road.
I will say the silence of sounds and movements;
the joy I know then will fall with seasonal rains
to touch and make again
the majestic spears and javelins of trees,
the ribbons of sunlight
the stones, along paths,
and velvet of flowers,
the fruit of the flourishing vine;
Rose and olive will touch again.

Fernando

Dear Fernando,
my own Fernando,
it is once again autumn and time for reflection;
your grapevine is in daily concert
with October sunlight, wind, and birds.
Are you standing tall, with eyes bright and step sure.
You were thus when we began battle together
all the many years ago.
Ours would be the sweetest and strangest
incense to burn,
the most noble and worthy ideas to consider,
and around us would stand, forever,
unique and devoted friends.
Unhappily,
with some gathering of days,
our harmony, with each other
and in the marketplace, did not play out
comfortably
so that we came to duel, often;
we selected our weapons,
mine, unhappy dolls,
yours, grievous spirits;
and in the early days, we won;
we lost, always, in the finishing days.

Now the drums are silent;
there is no flash of fire.
All that I can offer you
are these poor verses and their sentiment,
and, perhaps an ave.
But if you would be strong again,
and could walk beside me.
I would do it all again, Fernando.

from "Abba"

Angel Fire

In a space shaped by angels' wings,
I found you,
and you were as though I touched you,
like the voice of the violin,
or the gold in the waiting contralto.
And I came to let you be carried out away,
by those same angel wings.
There was left a burning coal in my breast,
so that I will not ever know an emptiness of
your roses' dew,
or the dimming to shadow of your nature,
not ever the suggestion of a musty pungence.
A moment is only a moment,
but its remembrance can be as the soft beauty
of your angels' wings,
thoughts that move and touch
with the intense duration of a burning coal.
Our somewhere, our colored appointment,
knows repose in that deep tempra
of flame, alive, within the burning coal.

Das Habicht Schrei

I heard the hawk's cry early today,
and I thought of you.
You are, both, far away,
but I was reminded
of your affection for this wild creature.
How much you admired its strength and carriage;
how much you wished to be as he.
And when you were wounded, mortally,
you struggled nobly with fear and conclusion;
and you bled for a great time,
finally to withdraw and die, silently,
eyes searching, on the ground.

Richard's identification with the hawk

Memory Garden

I walk now in hours and days of remembrance,
with morning fragrances,
with the joy of noontime,
in the falling steps of the afternoon.
It comes to me in song and touch,
and in wisdoms that reappear.
The wind wraps me in lost splendor;
shadows of leaves cover me in my want.
All of my space is as a nighttime memory garden,
with the gentle Pleiades
casing about their seven soft lights;
and lo,
in every illuminated presence,
I know reunion.

The pain tears and is lonely
tears came in a whirlwind of haunting melody,
and I knew my fatigue;
I have carried it like wealth amassed,
for a lifetime,
between our first blush and your burial grey.
I have gathered them all together,
the rhines of our days,
and with a sorrow
that wishes to be patience and shadowed,
I will allow tender, sympathetic flames
to take you to a comfortable distance.
Memories make possible the knowing
of the object loss,
but my days will not anymore permit
the frames, the conversations, the touch.
They have become as discolored rhines,
without fruit or flesh,
without surface and promise.
I do not wish, now, to hold a silk flower
and know the pain of sorrow
in the presence of a touch I have fashioned.
I have conspired against myself
and woven a great piece
that keeps me where I felt was nearer,
a fabric of rhines that no longer breathes.
Pain does not bring you
in necessary fullness to me,
and there is a growing separation
between my pain and your presence.

The duet is in voice singing
as though it were hushed and dim.
Straw covers where the tree stood;
and rhines, in their brown tones and decay
are welcomed by the earth,
bejeweling the soil
with colors out of yesterday.

Another Holding

What beauty out of a day of loneliness:
a romance of darkness,
a pledge in a single voice;
safety in grief passed leaves
hours filled with the passion of others,
their roses and melodies,
somehow then ours,
touching quiet reflections
of sunlight falling
onto yesterday's smiles and gifted bands.
Arranging in emptiness
and nothing finds again
the moment lost in its steps;
in the darkness
we catch wheat flying in the wind,
for its gold finds its grass
for our reaching hands,
and romance of another holding,
with pleats and ties,
hears with silent troth.

-Of Richard

Londonderry Reflections

Salute, Harold,
gentle declarations and loving compliments,
for over a great distance your voice rose to greet me:
of it was a roundness and a gold,
within, a quiet blessing.
Memory smote my heart,
and warmth struggled with the distance to you.
I weep with the soil that wraps you about,
for we are divided in our possession,
exquisite clay wanting of its ardor,
its spirit incorporeal,
breath out of devine alchemy.

The morning's softness
brought a bird's song in my chimney;
it was near, close,
and then I heard it as I flew upward and out,
away, away.
It was as though it captured your spirit
in the last years and days,
so that my heart caught to it
and was pulled away with it
like an unraveling grey ribbon.
The sound now is quiet,
and the ribbon is broken;
the chimney is dark and empty
except for the collected, shadowed memory
of the haunting benediction of the bird.

Sound and fragrance form the catalyst igniting my
grief,
and so,
haunting songs of the seasons
find yesterdays crowding into the sunlight,
winged crescendos into dessert greens,
above the playful arching of squirrels in new warmth;
the burning smoke of winder leaves
looks behind to a season of cold,
brothers letting go,
and gifts of small earrings;
and images collect
around the laughing melodies of summer,
perfumed in warm gardenia and honeysuckle.
The organ and horns,
the violin and piano,
and close, amaretto and hazelnut,
bring again hours to me now past,
and flowers stand as maids in waiting
to catch my tears
of sense and knowing.

When we have known great love,
and passed among many seasons,
we watch the hours of sunlight
as we would ledger the progress of days.
For the coming of night
is as that of the last, true dark,
and the image,
the likeness,
sets our hearts to ponder
and wish for a sure comfort.
The hours moved out of each other
into those of quiet,
and review;
And with warm memory,
only just now was the morning.
With a breathless anticipation,
when all things come to be;
the first roses are almost with us still,
and the ship of the day has sailed away
with the soft mimosa blossom;
but now, there is a distance to the roses
and we can see all that did not arrive,
to fall into our arms,
to be sewn into a pattern,
and so we, with the conclusion of the day,
and with warm memory,
allow our hope for new hours
in which we know,
or else a peace in which we do not know,
where flawless petals will fall,
their purity of sound,
unheard.

Cosmosic Anymore

I do not, anymore, wish, when tender
occasion and sentiment profuse,
the mercurial press of touch
or voice, nor image, in radiance light,
strength to rise, wisdom
to bind or free;
and with most reluctance, I mourn the
giving over all their joys,
painting out their passions,
to disciplined cleanliness,
all,
fragrances and colors, and fashioned
a mysterious beautiful,
all flowers under widest, gentle sky;
farewelling leaves, noble, outer sweetmeats,
emeralded movings, those yet
chartreuse,
those matronly thaeloed – these to be
distanced from me,
these reminding, surely, perpetual
summer,
innocent, fabled as always wandering, but
to its place, always,
parameters of cosmosic laughter,
that of romance, together, all, in warm radiance,
again.

A Small Season

Soft adagios held up the widening silk of dawn, with
rose against purple, lighted behind by
a metaphorical candle, it to become the full of day,
these hues promising cold, and November
bowing to the first chapter of winter
festival, coming December.
A hawk's cries remind, above the adagios,
a sad trumpet to the assemblage
of birds of chill.
My heart, my heart, rain begins,
soft notes in the dry waiting
expanse of brown
and gold, but more,
in my deep inward, it being somehow
good to remember, and for the all of it,
to weep, inside, companioning
crimson to gold, whose wet makes again alive,
and near, with fancied properties
which I can, however hold.

Elizabeth
November 16, 2003
6:30 – 7:00 a.m.
Sunday

Chrysanthemum Moment

Chrysanthemum moment,
into the vastness of lighted senses,
a season is fulfilled and realized,
journeying through night
from anticipation to revealing;
gold has torn open his heart
to offer his brilliant, most gold,
and crimson bleeds forth
from dark chambers of birth,
a rich wetness,
blackened blood,
deep and true.
Beside stand maids and groomsmen
who wait,
to catch golden tears
and to polish the crimson flow,
coming to complexion
some of those they serve,
rose Victoria,
talisman orange,
shyful French charteuse.
Great fans moving time,
mourning,
into today; yesterday, bashful,
beyond, reaching into tomorrow;
chrysanthemum moment,
hold,
until the color of your last,
crawling fig-like bud

has heard yesterday's calling;
let me know then in whose hands lie the fans,
who touches them,
through the gentle husbandman
who moves his bow
into lamentation for all that sorrowful.
Chrysanthemum moment,
coming into shadow,
and I do not,
cannot know the holder,
the candlestick to your splendor of the day,
your complete beauty with ephemeral wisdom
drawing each leaf and flower;
these would instruct,
but I cannot bear their lessons.
Immortal yearnings deny your portion,
chrysanthemum,
your moment that is passing into yesterday,
and I beg a blindness and a numbness,
to hang about,
to veil this knowing,
until gold has no heart,
and crimson has no blood,
until knowing grief
does not anymore pleasure,
and the fans have never been known,
nor shadow, chrysanthemum,
until their lamentations are quieted,
and beauty in yesterday is touched by hope,
becoming the calling voice of a tomorrow.

March thunder punctuates early, soft rain,
and emerging, jeweled green
gives heart to the lingering winter grey.
My lamps hold away amens,
but I have no hero today,
no loving tasks to carry through,
no exchange of words,
not enough strength to sit
with wounding, scarlet memory.
Perhaps I will ledger all of the good I know,
and place it beside a lighted candle
that I be strong in its fullness,
to find a peace in songbirds' beginning play.
I will take the entry of yesterday's sunlight
and fling it about the room
and, with small hurts softened,
find warmth inside the cold rain,
to touch lighted beauty before amens.

The Reflection

In the shadowed portion of the day,
I found flawless ivory
in the blossom from the lily of the valley.
Also was deep yellow softening,
like dusted pastry,
forming September's golden rod,
and royal purple has pushed up
and arranged into wild verbenia.
These came to die,
these thought-laden images,
running away and leaving a reflection,
removed, in a glass:
the petal quality of your skin,
the blush on your full lips,
and the olive of your fingers
that brought to me
an early morning's meadow bouquet:
rosemary lying happily with mist,
country orange close to peasant daisies.
And then the carriage of sound
took away their hues and forms,
and I was left with the lingering fragrance of memory,
its stones of grandeur a quiet echo,
falling within a still, haloed light.

Glow Everlasting

In the smoke that rises to you from mine,
its earthened chamber;
in the sunlight that falls from your smile
to my constant mourning,
within these there wraps covers, folds about my face;
the summer's gardenia and jasmine,
your breath of love, a passion fragrance.
Ripened fruits in autumn colors
offer their fullness to our celebration,
our feast of remembrance.
It does not matter that your hand
will not light the candle of layered tallow,
for my heart is yet on fire, with a glow everlasting.

Comingled

All of the beauty and sorrow
that struggle and embrace within any one heart
escapes my capture;
still I wish to somehow surround and contain that
selected with my words,
that others will know their wealth,
and reach out in what is a most primitive and exalted
endeavor:
to catch the longing to touch and know that two live
and feel rather than one,
that the butterfly and songbird color and sound the
mornings for two,
offering one romance with gold and melody.

Warmth Left

Summer dreamer within
the aria of summer softness,
finding summer ashes;
twilight that harkens to a silent voice;
the unknowing pendulum
and house whispers inside coming darkness;
there is not step,
no touch,
and friends forget olive and chestnut.
The summer twilight will hurry the darkness,
and the pendulum will continue into the last light;
moments pull with strength,
and knowing quietly weeps,
but the dream will find voice,
and step and touch,
for ashes hold warmth
left from deeply flamed coals.

Bittersweet Reprieve

A hawk's cry in the gathering August warmth;
the morning grows into its fullness,
and the truth of the day presses forth:
you are not here,
and cannot be.
You rise with the cry,
and I know your distance.
Years pass,
with the gold,
the heat,
the cry,
and you are not here.
But in the intimacy of the cry,
there is possible,
perhaps,
a wholeness,
for the strength of struggle in passion
knows a pause,
a quiet, bittersweet reprieve of time and distance,
with assurance that the hawk flies
in a space that catches echoes of life
and the governance of accepting memory.

Punctuation Rescinded

You did sleep,
and then, with a quick punctuation of it,
you did sleep unto finality.
I held your hand,
and you let go,
the last clasp.
It was done quickly,
and I knew suddenly a darkness.
A stretching out of time with anticipation
smoothed away into a nothingness.
You had been quiet in it all,
but the silence conversations, our last embraces,
now cry out
at their leave-taking and in their absence.
I cannot see you now,
but I know,
and that knowledge is like a brilliant portion
of hanging tapestry that shows us together,
the punctuation and all that was in it,
rescinded,
and our hands hold again each other.

After the Winter

The ministering salve of time
has healed my wound of you,
but to its side has left another.
Lost pain,
lost emptiness,
remembered rapture faded-
these open a portion of my heart
that, in a distanced sense,
cannot be consoled;
and the truest crimson bleeds out,
in a separate chamber,
that, with the distance,
it does not matter.
For like a season passed,
that of grief remains,
after the winter,
only as an echo
which cannot be touched.

A recognition of my gain, and loss,
in the matter of Richard.

And comes,
in time,
the first day of summer,
when the season sits
in new hours of enthronement,
glorious in her beginning officiate:
the day gives up the geranium's scarlet glow
and the permission of the sun
the distance that the heart can wander.
Quietness finds the gentle air of the wind,
the graceful,
elf-like dance of the butterfly;
-crepe myrtle softness over particulars
and dreams exciting and patient,
for the summer day of the dreamer is long,
his passion,
finding,
dying slowly,
with sweetness.
And so,
passed are seven summers;
again the dreamer,
the grapevine
does not anymore call out darkness,
nor the redbird a color for weeping,
but a now of ruby and green memory,
and sentiments true of Olive and Rose.

The Knowing

Finishing sunlight drew clouds,
pale-rosed,
iridescent pearl,
gathering in soft rounds,
hanging in the still, pastel sky,
as mountains rising out of a placid sea;
horses,
in silent conversation,
within new summer meadow,
found the maypole quietly put away,
full summer calling
in the adventuresome lighting of fireflies.
Voices and instruments find you,
in approaching anniversary,
and the pain transmutes
into nourishment to my soul,
for I am on the other side of easter,
death has risen into living memory;
but continuing, left-over steps know hunger,
and a thirst,
that are filled by the pain,
as it visits a closeness,
so that the years are not merely unrecognizable space,
an uncharted distance in which you have been lost.
Until, then, darkness shadows
the pale-rosed, iridescent pearl,
let me struggle,

let my anguish hold
a new, first knowing of each moment of your absence,
the sum of its loss,
that our tale was, indeed, true,
and touched with dark beauty.

The whippoorwill will leave the twilight
to enter the early children's dew,
to sing with the mourning dove a duet
eloquent and serene,
of intuition and acceptance.
Is there comparison true enough
that your presence may be drawn.
Every portion of sand would sponsor a word,
and each petal would give up its grace
that record be made.
The silver in the seams and veins of nighttime webs
will be gathered,
and cups will be filled with gold
from the month of June;
yet light from the sunlit leaf,
the joyful blossom;
water peaceful and the pirouette of the firefly-
all will be held,
the plume and ink to draw your likeness.
Ribbons of winter night
and deep blue sea roads may lend some of their
majesty
that conversation of you sound
about with strength and honor.
Oh olive,
with this paisley of beauty,
become,
and wrap around me this,
your fabric of life.

Idyls from Quiet Waiting

Late Summer Melancholy:

The clusters of grapes that dress your vine,
weep their shadows onto their leaves,
that you are not, cannot be here to look on and to
gently ravish them,
for thus the meaning in their existence is lost;
and they will be left to darken, to wither, and to fall,
never realizing the fancy you wished in them.

The Refreshed Memorial:

Betrothal stones and bands,
like gathering up all there was and is of two great
loves
and rearranging so as to enjoy still,
handling tenderly because the love is, in some part,
the wearing of a comfortable, familiar but precious
discovery and remembrance.

Elusive Gold:

A lot circle of gold, fashioned to enhance my face;
no manner of search offered any reward.
And then, I considered that quiet concern would yield
the gold.
And it was so, that some few days,
gave an unexpected discovery.

It may be that abundant concern covers much, even
the treasure,
the golden circle.

The Presence of Silk and Wool:

How elegant to wear silk under fine wool,
feeling tall and straight, graceful and able,
Anticipating thus nature's change.
Color and texture become worthy gifts that allow us to
feel regal,
to command reflections that include worth.
Pleasing benediction, that she did wear, in plums and
earthtones,
silk under fine wool.

Heaviness in August:

We feel the weight of August in its closed, great
warmth,
reminiscent of the rooms, in past times, that hosted fire
for ironing.
We are so far into summer that we cannot borrow
from the spring
the freshness we remember,
and the days are so without punctuation,
that we are almost unaware of the promise of autumn.
Our blossoms try to stand bravely, but we cannot enjoy
them fully,
knowing, almost as dark laughter,

that with the gold of harvest comes the brown of all
other.
Somehow, we must breathe deeply
and not give over so much to the mourning of the
summer's passing
as to the new promising autumn with its anticipation
of festivals and a conclusion
that itself ushers in still another new beginning.

Wisdom in the Pie Point:

The pie is a finer work with the point toward the guest.
Aunts are certain to know so, until the evenings and
days,
the years balance everything, and so,
the point is somehow forgotten,
being given over to those who, themselves, consider
matters
that reflect their wiseness.

Parting Blossoms:

In most recent days, I cast about for something
beautiful to restore and refresh.
I came, in some little time, to see my mother's casket
flowers.
They were beautiful, graceful,
being in color the blush of the cheek and the kiss of
snow.
There were many variations, and I remember
considering,

that I might have suggested overmuch.
But she was many variations, always of these colors,
and she was a deep and ample giving;
She loved beauty and reflected this love.
And so, I did not need to look afar; even in her farewell,
her beauty,
and all that was selected to accompany her,
became the image that covers all the years,
and leaves me restored and with the peace
that is in a newly, quietly opened flower.

Unhappy Perspective:

Our love did fill the earth,
for it colored all of the awareness I experienced,
the green of forest and the blue of sky,
the olive in your face and hands
and the dark chestnut in your eyes.
So much love is beautiful, but without perspective;
for when you went away, my world was not, anymore,
filled up,
and was, indeed, a place void and empty.
I was alone and came to understand somehow
that I must color everything once more,
that salvation could be found again, fashioned in me,
alone.

He Died Unto Himself...

He died unto himself, and I have come now to let him die unto me;
it has been of great necessity, since he, in himself, did die,
that I let him die in my feeling and memory, in image and touch.
There is memorial in the speaking of his name, in recalling his features,
yet in repeating his words of quick wit, in lifting the glass.
These abound, and so I do not now call upon myself to suffer a continuous fresh wound, for no life can come of it.
There is only to know and to say he has been.
The hand of death has nullified our vows;
and so, does death play lieutenant to my wish and sentiment!
With a weariness,
I would that the lieutenant require fealty of command and that it be so.

A weary sentiment regarding
Richard, probably late at night-

May Hurt

May hurt,
remembering beginning Olive firmness
with velvet intention;
May sunshine still,
still,
but without Olive velvet,
with whispers and shadowed glimpses
of days that came once
and were walked away;
May hurt,
with May sunlight
and Olive messages at every Olive turn;
Rose knows the chronicle of May
in closing with the hurt
of pressing Olive memory.

Richard and I were married
May 30, 1970 in Fitzhugh Chapel
on Millsaps Campus

Keepsakes

Knowing rebelled on silence
and I knew, finally,
that riding on my sleeve
was a need for the beautiful, the pleasant,
reminders of good in forms
that are delightful and joyful,
thoughts friendly to the senses,
without shadows and dark echoes
in their movement.
And so, there came to me a golden butterfly,
with jewels of color touching about,
and a pale white, satin unicorn,
his majestic crown pointing almost heavenward.
They played within the fragrant nectar
of flowers that embroider sweet memory;
gentle playfellows,
companions in joy and comfort!
You are that given already to me,
and stored with care,
to come again to me.
My bequest to you is my willing heart
that in your joy
you may pull upon me
the amiable warmth of June,
to be kissed into contentment
by the fragrant cape jasmine.
This joyful food, that heals and sustains,
was prepared by hands
that no longer fold or nod,

but the nourishment is yet strong,
ever containing and daily appropriate
to the favor of the sun;
for our lives,
when dressed in their fullest green,
are only the chasing of new fireflies,
turning around to hop-scotch,
to catch again the butterfly and the unicorn.

House Closing

Closing the house for three days,
the hurt in its solitude came as small suns
of youth and passion,
removed,
the intermezzo woven about duty and honor,
the wandering nocturne of dreams past.
And so,
these guests of aloneness
romance unbroken quiet
to offer dialogue that draws tears
and dark smiles
so that the heart must close to them,
embracing a greater solitude,
but that without pain and mourning,
only that,
with the pattern fixed,
an emptiness flavored of campari.
-And the house can be opened again.

What of listening, deep into the night,
to the old masters,
with the splendid storm
of expression from their instruments.
These accomplishments stand
as elevated gold,
that we accept humbly
and what we can, of them, bring inside.
I listen and allow my thoughts to run away,
beyond my formulated ideas,
and just for a moment,
I fancy that I know.
All at once I can understand where the sky is,
why the sunlight in October touches and moves us
in a fashion that is different from that in July,
and, somehow, if souls are, indeed, living
when we are not thinking of them.
Most, I know that love remains,
for echoes, though distant, return,
again and again, and true.

Holyhock Stain

In love the whole is the heart's kingdom,
as the blue of sky,
its fullness,
thought encompassed with a glance.
The tarnishing of the sun,
eruptions from within,
expressing arrangements rare;
the darkening of evening shadows
-these are not inside,
alone with themselves,
but pattern acceptance,
yielding blossoms opening to touch,
the design, in completeness,
for its selection and enjoyment.
The borning of the day brings delicious variety
within its elegant same,
to offer the hollyhock leaf,
handsome and without fraternity,
to add to the salad
of elite and proud identities:
but in its beauty haute french: "high, elevated"
an humbling through
the power of the posture
and closeness of its fellows:
to stand with the hollyhock,
against a camaraderie
of circumstance and will,
positioned true,
with vision courting wisdom,

to know love
and the whole richness given to the hand,
touching the heart,
but patching stain withal its parts.
Without the gentlest wisdom
in your careful words,
those whose sting,
in selected, desolate moments,
a diminishing unto death-
without the gold,
quite turned apart from dark,
your flesh would not have made warmth,
and mine to yours,
an empty response.
The heart's wealth is wide and deep,
and in its wholeness
is offered a covering for nakedness
that comes to clothe
without these dissonant gifts.
The fateful distance I came,
let me begin again.

-My conclusion, Summer, 2000

In Richard's Sometime Understanding

In the newest hour announced, in a September day of
grey,
conforting an untold wish, I must say of love, and the
holdings
of my heart, that they silver downward, about as the
waterfall,
clear, as seen through of sunlight, so that in the tint of
gold,
only faintest hue, falls the bittersweet of all of my now
knowing;

Of others, the sounds of the lute, the piano and the
Hebraic violin,
yet the heavy beauty of the organ's voice – these may
be unheard
but they ring in to me, as Christmas bells in winter, the
mourning
to be touched, lifted out of its repose, to weeping of
that held,
only to lose in this the smallest cosem of us all; while
with others,
the darkness manifests as only an acceptance
requiring no
struggle of the thought of it.

But I, in confession, fancy the binding weeping of
others, not any
heaviness on these beyond the accumulated weight to
shoulders

dressed to their finding, I, only not to dance the sting
of fragile
happenchance, alone, but hands to reach, offering the
solace
of hearts that mirror my own, and in this seeing,
becoming dewfall,
graceful clouds moving, wandering, prayers sounding
in their upward
finding, beauty out of loss, together.

Elizabeth, 9/19/2001
After breakfast, following a tense rainshower which,
as a man, who comes into understanding, has
become soft – oh, Richard –

Sayings

The Increasing

Please, please, do not rest just now in
only the long ago; come – come, come
again, even within bittersweet
tears; touch me with your golden
voice, and tender my face with
your hungry, speaking fingers,
Olive loving, with new sweetness,
his faithful, abiding Rose.
Let spring furnish our chamber, its promise,
the bed to our warmth; let us turn a
second road, the first where
found love haloed by summer's radiance,
even a thousand white gardenias
whose fragrance has followed the
winds, the grail of growing
years, grieving me in this moment,
a thousand white gardenias that
stood morning into evening, their
only will to mirror love's first
season to Olive and Rose.

-Lost, and lost, found by kindly chance among
the scramble of reason and sentiment;
let then, these, my tears be gathered into a vessel of sculpted angel
coral,
etched with wandering ivory veins,
let these arrange,
that of the fragrance of a thousand
white gardenias, the surely continuing soul
of that first love, be breathed into at every
recognition of the increasing long ago.
3-14-2007

In Fair Linen

I do not wish new green,
the maiden butterfly,
Eden's light in the dragonfly's wing:
rather let the first green smile
out into the sunlight,
the elder butterfly curtsy to me her colors,
the forgotten dragonfly show again
the various daytime, lighted hues.
Let the longing of the journeyed heart
find images carried through
a pattern of a thousand golden days,
borne again on the faces of blade and leaf,
that seasons lost be found again
in the rhapsody of new openings,
in the wonderment of travail
that pushes forth a retelling,
to be wrapped about in new vestments,
a beauty within the fair linen of memory.

"Fair linen" is the new cloth placed
on the alter each Sunday before communion
in the Episcopal Church – often lovely.
I used to have after duty and changed it.

A Small Benediction

The quiet came like an absence,
a knowing suddenness;
Light fell at a distance,
as that forgotten,
and all else is a wanting.
The hurt is gone,
and its housing is empty,
and so, there is, in the balance, nothing.
All sound is asleep,
and laughter falls about in summers passed;
the afternoon is like a stone
inside a shadow,
a lily in a photograph,
the word speaking silently from its page.
–This record,
a small benediction that forgives the day.

Losing, gradually, silently pain of loss,
and its accompanying emptinesses.

A Shaped Dark

The stretching out of the afternoon's melody
was beauty patterned again,
of your distance,
and today,
a recognition that love can be,
in its fullness,
only so long as memory,
as true only as the day's commitment.
Red clover stands without color in the night,
and the moon can find its roundness,
alone,
without its crimson;
and so,
I know, in the moon's light,
your distance,
its round greatness,
but our crimson does not now reveal,
being left,
the distance filled
with a somehow reverenced emptiness,
a form waiting,
full of shaped dark.

In the cup left alone of the shyful kiss,
lie the leaves in ochers and raw
and burnt seinnas, their fire cooled,
their sentiment deeper, but
cloudy of their warmth;
eternity looks backwards, his "Pathitique"
still beautiful in absence of sixteen winters.
Where in the leaves lie the crimson
of the heart –
in the stain they show in the cup's
walls, of color dim, but in presence still,
a line that turns round the space
of the cup, back to itself –
we apart are still all together,
Arthur's final mummerings resonating
across the ages.

Elizabeth
February 17, 2009
Ten o'clock
Greg's birthday, music lovely, saying
Goodbye to a beautiful day of the
Heart –

Our days come in on crescendoing moments,
to exit in the finishing denouement of
accepted twilights;
and between these, we experience,
through multicolored sensings and polite
knowings, our bequeathed hours.
We forget into yesterday, and are buoyed
up by dreams found in the prefacing
tomorrows, these steps repeated through
industries that fill what becomes,
in eventual assessment, a poet's histoire.
We come to know that we are not
ever in the morning moments, or those
of twilight's softness,
but rather in the fluid reality between the
gatherings of each; and we, like a
river to the sea, mount, as on wings of
eagles, fatigued, but with our petite foxes
tamed, to enter the window to
that great, dark night.

Elizabeth
March 19, 2010
A beautiful, early spring day, now about nine-thirty pm
Images with me since yesterday, calling
to be penned tonight – Richard in my thoughts:
holy scripture I quoted to comfort him,
The Petite Prince, Rilke –
So far, the road back –

Brought Early

I brought music early,
and with cola and toast dressed with raspberry,
in the defenseless struggle with rising's fatigue,
with difficult drinking
from the well of night's restored excitement
and rested energy,
the sounds caught my heart,
finding a poignant ambiance of hands,
with casual, tender intimacy
searching out mine,
resting with a consented, silent,
almost boastful possession, on my thigh.
And I wept,
my lashes quickened and refreshed,
and in the innocently watchful sunlight,
I sat to wait the passing,
knowing again,
perhaps with a more studied, fundamental
clarity,
what of it I have kept:
love and new passion,
as in first summer,
in its long, generous hours,
when warmth and gardenias open mornings,
in reflection reveal the long
of the circumstance of consummation
so that there is press to move beyond,
into the night of doing and lost expectancy,
and the indignities of tense.

-Weeping and bearing the moment,
finding and acknowledging record,
warm blood saved,
pouring from a silent window in my heart.

Our passions have their seasons,
and I am in Autumn but
in reflection and
responses called out, I am,
in the loss of green, wet
and fresh, bound gold, the
moisture of feeling gathered.

Addendum

There is, perhaps, some wisdom
in knowing the beauty and worth
of the tears we allow to fall,
for when they are of regret and loss,
they ask for the strength
of some of the passion in our hearts,
falling like many colored jewels
into a physical world that is,
on some wise,
foreign to our spirits.
It may be that the tears of angels
are, alone, altogether acceptable,
neither yet those of
humble beasts or gentle flowers;
being angels their tears are completely beautiful,
for they are shed in our stead.
It can be that one angel's tear
can spill onto another's weeping eyes,
so that what was dark can become light,
what is lost,
wonderfully found,
and that which was desert, again beautiful,
a divine garden, yet a paradise.
We do not, then,
require the great portion of our tears,
for we are all, none,
not any, greater than another.
It is therefore not wise or happy
to consume ourselves, with ourselves,
and to be left lacking and undone.

When trees have quieted
and move only where there is light,
when the stream is not speaking,
but flowing without sound,
when lilies and roses have become playful
and have breathed their fragrances
into the still, warm air,
and when I exchange carefully, reverently,
the veiled lamp for the bright lamp in the mountain,
the season is to gather and to close;
I count my wounds and gifts,
and then there is no will
to approach the matter of my aloneness.
There is an arrangement now, a completeness,
a conclusion, and I am weary.
This is a busy unfolding,
this matter of the day,
and well, as if there are no misadventures,
that our fighting cocks
always emerge deadly accurate,
with smooth, red blood,
flowing and warm.

Tomorrow I will get to my grieving.
I will carry it always, but as a shadow.
Only on good days will I open it to the light,
and look full into it.

Is this not the means of losing recognition and
relationship,
a strange arrangement which does not anymore
evoke our first sentiments.

Ah! – To Begin

In the last hours of darkness,
I observed the coming of the day.
The plenitude of sunlight at last
touched each expression of nature,
and the dew included everything with its freshness.
I thought,
how happy is the first portion of the day,
promising and expectant.
I chanced to hear from the radio an intermezzo,
the violin and piano pulling forth great emotion.
At once I felt all the beauty and sorrow of my life
come inside my heart with the music.
The pain was a deep heaviness,
and I bent.
Again I thought: am I at the finishing of the day?
Is there no more promise;
are there left no other grande expectations?
Can it be that the rhapsody has played out.
Is the golden bowl, my troubled soul, broken?
Will my spirit be lifted away,
to take on the fragile natures of memory and song.
It may be that I will not stand as the heath,
achieving presence and character
simply by continuing.
Unhappily, in this consideration,
I require a golden bounty in all my harvests.

I want to go where love is;
I want to feel what love is.

Taken from the song
"I Wanna Know What Love is"
by Foreigner.

Second Suddenness

Some light rain has fallen,
its cadence soft upon the rigid but accepting straw.
I grasped and held to the freshness in the outdoors
as I approached the partially opened bedroom door.
Beauty conspiring with me,
I was back and safe,
quite forgetting the unhappy moments just before,
safe until the hour, when pressed,
that the darkness steals me away again from myself.
Coffee is wonderful and dark now;
the ornaments of peace and quiet are in place.
In a second suddenness,
my symphony is begun again,
the entire orchestration full and harmonious.

The Moment of the Organ

The music of the organ is altogether grande,
like the moving of a dark wind
and the falling of great waters.
Yet within its sounds
is found the echo of the butterfly's wings
and the sign of the tired, brown-stained cape jasmine.
It is as the nighttime sky,
a sweeping, serene vastness
including smiling, knowing stars.
And you come to me with the organ's music,
and you make a full-toneness,
a mahogany of the soft lightness
to the larger darkness,
so that I almost know rose tones.
And so there are tears
but theirs will be a quickened shadowing,
for the nighttime sky gives over to the day,
with only reminiscence of stars and tears,
and reason, with deliberate movements,
steps into the old leather of sentiment.

In hours passed, those that have,
and are shaping my now,
I chose to do that which I wished,
the yearnings of my heart,
the clasping passions of my soul;
in those moments, those steps and reachings –
in those times and settings –
those behaviors, each, seemed the most right,
the best of all offered,
the good my inner self so earnestly
sought.
In this circumstance, when my hair was
raven, when my motivations
were innocent, when joy in living was a
bright jewel, intermittently blinking,
laughingly calling to me, a joy with only
outward shadows –
in this circumstance, how was I to know: in
this recognition, then, lies my peace.

It was not just the best I could do, it was all,
the only that I could do.
Such is being in isness; and we need not
to look at the inner shadows too long,
less they become judgments out of season.

Elizabeth
September 11, 2009, first entry
The best summation I could manage in a
very difficult, deepest night –

Having risen early, I remembered the
very profusion of unproofed verses
I had begun editing in the
late night, finding our expressive song:
it became a thoughtful treasure
to carry as I walked the stairs down;
under the candle's bloom, it became a
passionate, impeting source, allthewhile
dying in my hand; dry tears burst forth, to fall
with the hued shadow of glory spreaded about
by bronze and gold chrysanthemums.
Elgar sounded beautifully, and with the small industry
of carrying the vacuum out, the music was more
beautiful in the dark, in the distance –
and when I closed the storeroom door,
I paused, to touch again, to be certain of the
lock.

Elizabeth
October 12, 2009
About five o'clock am

And in the night, in company with
wandering, seeking steps,
my glance fell inside his modest
study; I say, at once, that
one of the dried roses had fallen,
and I knew that he was lost,
but, more, that my heart, in this
knowing, was not silent.
The night drew close around me with
the knowing, and I felt my steps to
quieten,
for I had found a gift, and with it,
I wept,
my tears, in help, imaging
a thousand white gardenias.

Elizabeth
April 2, 2009
About four o-clock am
Richard's sixty-sixth birthday, coming
April 4 –
So far away, now, those beautiful, fragrant
white blossoms of summers
passed –

A Richard Dream

The unhappy visit of the night before
was pressed into work and thought
quite away from its
romancing images, clear, but as
dark
silver, troubling, your body, horizontal,
as on a bier, the bedding
surely calling the shroud;
your arm, lifted, two poor fingers, extended
toward the kindly beast – mister
who softly stated that they must the
sacrificed,
and then left would be less, find less than
half left.
The images passed, all in the brown of
leather, the grey of rising smoke,
as the changing seasonal hue of green,
in the humble form of the pushing blade, the
noble needle to the pine;
the words a dialogue in thought
aware, in pain thought it be
forgotten,
and into eventually
I look, I think in memory, touched,
its colors pleasant, and truly

providing,
but we remain, always, just
for the moment,
solemn when we approach the dark at the
top of the stairs.

Transcribed
October 30, 2002

Valentine's Eve

2007

I watched the night fall, and heard
beauty, finding softest pink
carnations drifting with
the ear, these long-stemmed blossoms
lying at my morning door,
I having passed the night in his rooms,
he, forgetting his thoughtfulness,
I, not requiring, and so gently
surprised and pleased.
I looked into the new, covering dark,
and saw only, greatly, the dark,
but with a patient, treasured
grief, knew the silent images of
first love, intense and stumbling,
yet graceful in its innocence.
In the dark of the evening's continuing
innocence, and in the dark of
growing memory, its filling
introspection finding a haunting
acceptance,
held, abiding, fire, inside a thousand white
summer-warmed gardenias, these hanging close inside
forever
fire that once burned,
whose flames shown wet
scarlet and bleeding crimson centered
of rosed talisman orange and

passion's gold; this fire echoes in
the evening stillness so that the dark quivers
with its visitation, these movements
casting of lights, as upon flowing
water, of scarlet and crimson,
rosed talisman orange, and passion's gold,
lifting a fragrance of summer-warm
dying gardenia, ecrued, and,
exempting comparison,
a heart's gift,
a delicate confection, offering
sweetness as the lark's voice ascending.

After Valentine's

2007

This morning after Valentine's; drinking
Richard, from his cup, English china
brought from across, pheasants and
nice borders; and anniversary touches;
hard, mamma coming to, at last,
rest, her myriad fears quieted,
but in their quieting,
the calling away her voice and touch,
her simple wisdoms, gentle as a
warm coverlet for her own, in whatever
difficult climes.
Not again, since, has been seen so lovely
a gathering of blossoms as those
selected for her service;
and Richard, Richard, your balsm and
red are imaged true, in these moments
of drink and reflection:
two loves, abiding still, in selected
moments of new heavy grief,
but today, in sunlight as distant
as your smiles, my toys of
china and flower images, their
colors true as blossoms in my
hand,
these find an ephemeral joy, the
cup's pheasant looking out of its
finely drawn, brown cloak,

253

surely, thine, your chestnut taken
form, speaking a poignant
greeting and goodbye,
these that struggle to hold in time's constant thievery.

2-15-2007

Dreameyes

Daring true has come through a moment's
gold, its filling darkest chestnut
pools which held certain
recognition;
but I must learn the words and sounds
of signatured truth, and not that of
sweet sentiment, pulsating still smiles,
those given to me, as they first were, hearing
tonight's soft rain as tears stored
and dark, gathered,
each as it fell, its universe of
hurt and loss kissed into
the heart's capture and deepest keeping;
dark pools of quieted chestnut paradox, still,
first and last devotion, dressings
to the middle, fallow whole,
whose emptiness leaves from this
poor record in knowing morning
light, burden familiar, its grey,
echoing heaviness,
the ginger lily's aura not fully
caught, but drifting in and
away, these of burden alive, and
wounding as glances
that, with their piercing swords of scorn,
struck unto death, my innocent,
questioning – begging heart.

2-9-2007
In a night of dreams of Richard's eyes.

255

You wished the good,
but could not,
whether of prophecy, sign
or loosed demons,
reach it,
and so you pushed me
in the directions, all, which you could not follow.
I felt some care from you,
that you chose me
to be your vessel, by proxy, of truth and good,
to perhaps approach what you could not attain.
In the all of it, we both became, together,
more good than before.
That I reason so calls me to gratitude,
for in a great sense, a portion of my worth,
however humble, is a gift of you,
your leading and fashioning,
being always there, in the shadows, with the script,
while I carried forth the instructions,
to completion,
in the sunlight,
supported by your dark strength and knowing;
it was a time, if not of love, of courage and hope.
And so I speak to you, now, in voice,
to tell you that your effort is, in the unfortunate
backward glance,
a review without touching, acceptable,
that your heart, through mine
is, at last, realized as worthy and good.

Now that the struggle is done,
could the riddle be simply unraveled
by considering that all of the
advice, instruction, pressing-
have been to work a certaintude
that I would embrace
his theoretical self,
his very soul,
and with my acceptance,
then to walk through his impotent postures.

Of the river and the tender reed;
of love and the delicate, razored wound;
of the sensitive nature and the burden of resolve;
to his dreams, how near the chariots of fire.

- Elizabeth

New Bloom

Is there hope enough,
a promise perhaps of love,
that I might cause the lamp again to bloom;
or find blossoms that grasp each other's petals
and dance in multi-colored laughter;
will the wind pass its bow
through the handsome cedar's fir
and make a delight of the violin
that I can know;
or can the faithful raindrop
find the already verdant meadow,
to sound her rare, gentle silence-
and I will know.
The hands part and gather,
but it is in the heart that beauty is placed,
by another,
that escaping the cutpurse
and allowing the touch
which becomes the bloom of the lamp.

The Sentence

The sentence of decisions past, and ill thought,
is falling quickly now upon me;
September coming, and close,
will bring the beginning of finishing seasons,
and I am unable to be brave, to bear their truth.
Regret and a reflective pity wound,
Alternating with a peace born in tired acceptance.
I have escaped nothing, but wandered with will,
yet innocently, into the dark.

An assessment, fall 2000
And again, perhaps, more so, October 2001, reviewed.
2002

The Separate Grief

Of it all, moments into hours play
out the script of given circumstance,
of event and purpose,
requiring, taking;
and while, in these, grief softens,
in new wholeness,
in the freedom of it, rises
a separate grief, that, in the wholeness,
the wound healed over,
the scarlet pulled together,
we are left, in our newness, lessened
the slightest hue,
tones arranged into a kind
distance, images softly shadowed,
and threads of honor
borne away on the wind.

Bound Innocence

So slow is eventuality,
innocent in its coming reminders,
how clever its larger closet, its screen and drape.
Of our own will there arrange,
and so with surprise hear the tale of truth,
and accept our lesser strength.
And we speak of the journey into ourselves
as beginning, still, with greatest wisdom
to be found in some distant season,
its colors not quite clear,
with no suggestion of our having
already passed through.

Elizabeth 2001

It was in the little things that I first
found your love, and this knowing has
come back to me tonight,
without announcement or thought, but
as an image of your selecting
clothing for a day of work: you touching
the fabrics, the uncluttered glance
toward them, quite unaware of your demons
and their press.
So real is the image that I am taken back to
those first days, those of gardenias,
even, yes, a thousand of them, but I do not
stay, my hand catching my throat.
The sentiment is passing with the image, but I
am thoughtful all over again of the
Strange circumstance that came to be –
Roses to whom we were, lovers, then to
become predators to each other's soul while
showing, simultaneously, as
buttresses, strong, for each other's
needs.

The song is full of dark, the gardenias
most beautiful, remembered, but I cannot
forget that they bloomed when you first smiled,
quietly, touched, hesitantly, cared, in some
fashion, for a soul sick unto death,
becoming fire to your passion, to eventually
turn its flame toward my undoing,
and not toward my bed.

Thoughts and thoughts – a lifetime of them,
and you still color the small, most inward ones.

Elizabeth
October 26, 2009, early evening
An image of Richard, quickly passing, but igniting
much sentiment and memory--

In deepest night, I stood under the
lamp, and to my left glance,
unexpectedly, yellow daisy rounds
of sunshine hued petals and chartreuse
centers slowly blinked out to me.
His once kept Edelweise, became dark brown,
glass marbles, inside the moving lights
of chestnut that played about his
hair.
My senses usurped my thought, and a
sudden libation of a tender
moment, generously his presence,
moved quickly past, a golden moment,
to become a profusion of summer daylight,
punctuated by fragrant gardenias, a very
thousand of them.
And I knew a personally arranged wisdom –
that given to us lesser gods –
the heart loves in part, the whole,
and to protect, semantics fail, but feeling
is staid, however in reflection, yet
perpetual.
I stood, upon my plains of Carthage, again,
real and true.

Elizabeth
In deepest night, February 3, 2010
A passing apparition of Richard on wings of gathered yellow
daisies – I do not wish so, but the sentiment
is present with the strength of its repression –
How dear the veil of distance through unquestioned absence –

During evening prayers,
I offered up thanksgivings and
with sweet herbs and cedar
I asked for strength.
And then I came to remember those of mine,
gone away, lost to me as they once were.
I begged for their peace, and as I formed my thoughts,
a sensation of dark water came upon me,
so that I could not breathe.
And so, for a brief time, a time of soft light,
I did not pray for their peace.
This is the way: we step into the grave with them,
and then we step up and out, to throw in the soil resting
on the grave's side, and perhaps place a flower.
Such is our romance with life.
Loss swallows itself up, and our dialogue with our lost
ones
though grief is lessened and in some fashion,
concluded.
A small round ball of sorrow and grief rolls out away
from us to a safe distance,
until another thought, another prayer, another closing
of a grave,
spills out more unhappy feelings.
Choruses of trumpets cannot bring them back,
and their graves soon become empty.
And so, we grieve but only so that we feel a painful
closeness,
then to retreat into silence to let it bathe us
as a healing lotion that will allow us to walk again,
to pick up again the ball of sorrow.

First Soul Apart

The morning sun brings a new greeting,
more the distance today to you,
and with the twilight,
a quiet goodbye,
companioned to accepted dark
without your hand.
Flowers have forgotten to offer lesser blooms,
spreading forth a beauty abundance,
or is my eye now,
weary of tears,
knowing beauty,
that with patience,
kept her colors silent
until I could hear them separate of you.
Forever began when you closed your voice,
and is divided into seasons;
through green and dust,
and gold and chill,
you wander still away,
and with the sunset over budded leaf,
that beyond vine and fruit,
or flame against rusts and umber or winding smoke,
your smile ever still becomes as they,
my heart to hold you, yet,
though in their company,
first soul apart.

-my composite sentiment of Richard,
arrived, Autumn 2000

Song Enough

Suddenly the day rushed forth to meet me,
thrusting awareness upon me,
decrying fancy,
hard reality passing out of shadow
into innocent sunlight.
The fullness of day spoke into the newness,
foretelling violet shadings
to hang about the beauty of flowers,
a sadness to find hearts that open to the gentle,
pressing curiosity of light.
The wisdom in this foreboding,
coupled with a growing meditation of joyful finding,
left the cloth of the day spread out,
to receive,
knowing that the strength of it
will play out into melodies that fail our dreams;
but the day touches,
inviting compelling adventure,
a pilgrimage,
its struggle and prayers,
its laughter content,
hours of playful origami,
-in its history will be song enough.

Vanished Dew

It was easy,
at the first,
to be sentimental,
to remember tones of voice and smiles.
There was necessity to collect words,
and arrange them,
to pen lovely portraits.
Now, with the poverty of years,
there is only,
when loss is again discovered and looked into,
most,
a distant, dark emptiness.
The stone, speaking Rilke,
and flowers,
remind that,
in each day following,
I need remember only the light from vanished dew.

Again, one of my many
assessment/attempts to place
Richards's memory in my
feelings –

Conclusion

The time was after the storm,
and the moon shown forth;
there was a full orchestration of
gray and light, yet a soft glow,
like a gathering of ivory satin brushed
with dark fern;
and without, lay a quiet stillness that sang
nature's sovereignty.
In these moments, I fancied my heart
did not beat, and I quickly reviewed my loss:
would my praise to the jeweled butterfly,
touching about the spider's night
embroidery,
no longer be raised; would I forfeit the
words from the golden treasury of morning
songbirds; and would my glance
not anymore fall on the diamonds of dew
as they laughingly climb the sun's
rays into heaven.
At different junctures, we take, as I did take, my
heart into my hand, to decide to walk the
distance or give in to the despair of loss,
whatever its fashioning.
In my hand lay my heart, and in its quiet lay
conversation with you; and I wept with the
thought.
And so I took my heart to a chapel to pray,
that flowers and arched moonlight
offer me conclusion.

In the beating of my heart is my knowing,
so that I cleave to my songbirds and sunlight;
I will wait, then, until the feast is complete, to then
enter into a dialogue of reunion,
two wayfarers who walk the same path.

Elizabeth (in revision)
a very early piece, a time of many losses, sparring
with dark thoughts –

The warmth of the past is with us,
always,
playing the delightful game of dance,
arms about,
and then free;
almost to touch and losing to the moments,
the music of memory
calls up beautiful treasures
wrapped in a blend of sunlit and nighttime colors.
Helpful is to draw the silhouette in the distance;
it is the silken hue we see in gathered roses,
and it is the poignancy in everyday fragrances;
it is the slow promenade of narrative
that winds through our dreams;
it fills up the shadow
so that the grey becomes familiar friend or kin,
and it is the hurting rapture in the innocent symphony.
It is never complete,
but is the cup that runs over into abundance;
that of it not warm is left to torture us,
in words unheard,
only intention hanging about like a clear cloth,
to wound with its cold, pallored silence.

How sweet the quiet
of content,
that of holding,
remembering,
dreams of fancy,
or,
perhaps most, the likeness
of repose
in acceptance,
with the wealth of will
left over.

Elizabeth,
May 16, 2008
5:45 am

I Give Thee

I give Thee, my love,
The dust of the rose,
The brief adventure of the snow,
The peace of the night's
closed light.

That you are idea, a dreamthought,
I have secret certitude
that in your hand rests a gift: perhaps,
one, the color of the sun; another, the passion
in geranium red; more, the very constancy
of the seasons themselves.

Elizabeth, July 27, 2009

If I can have the day,
on the proclamation of new
morning, I will be grateful;
for the hour, the very moment,
I am, even now, joyful.
There is no loss so great that,
in full knowing,
its emptinesses are truly real.
In life, in awareness is the season
of romantic spring,
its hope, its towardwards glance
to summer's radiance.

Elizabeth
April 18, 2010

I pen my thoughts,
in large measure for myself,
as examination
of the powders and dews of my soul;
more, I pen my thoughts
that they might become a humble buttress
for others,
whose exclamations
are left unattended and unsoothed.
I write more of beauty and hurt
and less of ugliness and redemption.
Often in my morning lines,
the idea and supporting metaphors
show dark passion and despair,
but whether of fancy or a rejection of what is,
victory becomes the closing construct.
Perhaps victory is so often written in for me
because, simply, I have a faith
that was kindled when my hair was raven
and my eyes were open wide to experience.
This faith has shown me,
in every circumstance I can remember,
the new silver behind the old darkness,
and the fluid gold in the morning following the night.

It can become a burden, however,
to see the truth,
to know the honorable and good.
And so, there are moments
when I cannot play out the wisdom
I have come to know.
My pen becomes the better of my voices,
speaking of what ought to be
and not of what is.

Valediction

How does one close the door on an experience which so wounded that its dimensions are without measure. One simply does not, but looks past them to the morning, when all things are again new. The wound and its many unhappy qualities can be explored whenever the heart is ready and able to review. Otherwise, the distance between the wound and the morning is the balm, the work of the Samaritan who crossed over to help and heal.

One does not forget the matters of the heart, but draws distance between the matter and its held sentiment. Looking to morning, looking past, looking beyond is the glory of the impetus we are each slave to, each day, to rise with will, toward light.

Elizabeth
June 24, 2010

*"For all that has been, thanks;
for all that will be, yes!"*

Dag Hammarkjöld
Secretary to the United Nations
1943 to 1957 Intermittently

Harold and Agatha
1970-1992